MAKE MARKET LAUNCH IT

The Ultimate Product Creation System for Turning Your Ideas into Income

By Pam Hendrickson & Mike Koenigs

http://www.MakeMarketLaunch.com

© **2012 Product Solutions Group, LLC. All rights reserved.**

No part of this publication may be reproduced or transmitted in any form or by any means, mechanical or electronic, including photocopying and recording, or by any information storage and retrieval system, without permission in writing from the authors (except by a reviewer, who may quote brief passages and/or show brief video clips in a review.)

Disclaimer: No portion of this material is intended to offer legal, medical, personal or financial advice. We've taken every effort to ensure we accurately represent these strategies and their potential to help you grow your business. However, we do not purport this as a "get rich scheme" and there is no guarantee that you will earn any money using the content, strategies or techniques displayed here. Nothing in this presentation is a promise or guarantee of earnings. The content, case studies and examples shared in this book do not in any way represent the "average" or "typical" member experience. In fact, as with any product or service, we know that some members purchase our systems and never use them, and therefore get no results from their membership whatsoever. You should assume that you will obtain no results with this program. Therefore, the member case studies we are sharing can neither represent nor guarantee the current or future experience of other past, current or future members. Rather, these member case studies represent what is possible with our system. Each of these unique case studies, and any and all results reported in these case studies by individual members, are the culmination of numerous variable, many of which we cannot control, including pricing, target market conditions, product/service quality, offer, customer service, personal initiative, and countless other tangible and intangible factors. Your level of success in attaining similar results is dependent upon a number of factors including your skill, knowledge, ability, connections, dedication, business savvy, business focus, business goals, and financial situation. Because these factors differ according to individuals, we cannot guarantee your success, income level, or ability to earn revenue. You alone are responsible for your actions and results in life and business, and by your use of these materials, you agree not to attempt to hold us liable for any of your decisions, actions or results, at any time, under any circumstance. The information contained herein cannot replace or substitute for the services of trained professionals in any field, including, but not limited to, financial or legal matters. Under no circumstances, including but not limited to negligence, will Pam Hendrickson, Mike Koenigs, Product Solutions Group, LLC. or any of its representatives or contractors be liable for any special or consequential damages that result from the use of, or the inability to use, the materials, information, or success strategies communicated through these materials, or any services following these materials, even if advised of the possibility of such damages.

ISBN: **978-0-9888663-0-0** (paperback)
ISBN: **978-0-9888663-1-7** (epub)
Library of Congress Control Number: **2013901920**

Published by:
Product Solutions Group, LLC.
3830 Valley Centre Drive, #705-314
San Diego, CA 92130

866-654-6534 or 858-720-8720

Dedication

To anyone who has ever had a dream to make the world a better place through your unique knowledge, wisdom and experience.

May this book provide the pathway for you to turn your passion into reality and in the process create the income, impact and legacy you desire.

"Nothing is withheld from us which we
have conceived to do. Do things that have
never been done."

—Russell Kirsch, inventor
of the programmable computer

Table of Contents

A Note from the Authors

I was drawn to the training and development industry because of the magic that happens when someone's life is transformed. Probably like you, however, I got here in a roundabout way.

I grew up back East in a small town in western New York: Corning, NY. My dad was a process engineer for Corning, Inc.—a Fortune 500 company—for 40 years, and my mom was a church organist and piano teacher who changed thousands of teachers' and students' lives through her work, lecturing around the world about how to empower children to learn.

My mom and my dad worked hard to support me, build my confidence and give me an amazing education. They sent me to Brown University, where I graduated *magna cum laude* with a degree in psychology. My plan was to use my degree and my background to help others in the same way as my mom had.

Through a series of crazy events (more on that another time!), I ended up in California where I had the chance to work for the Anthony Robbins' organization. Working with Tony Robbins for almost 18 years, in what ultimately became the role of Vice President of Content and Product Development, gave me an incredible opportunity to experience firsthand the power of creating products and services that transform people's lives. I learned both from my own experience (which included plenty of mistakes!) and from seeing the impact the company's products and services had on our customers—as well as on the sustained growth in the business as a result.

I left soon after my mom had passed on. I not only felt the pain of her loss, but realized I was missing out on precious time with my family and two little boys because of the intense schedule my job required. I also wanted to continue her legacy in a more personal and meaningful way.

I started to wonder what would happen if I could take everything I had learned from my mom, and from my time at the Robbins organization, and use it to help others create products and services that make a difference—to extend the processional effect that my teachers had on me.

Shortly thereafter, I met Mike. He was incredibly intriguing to me. Not only is he a graduate of almost all of Tony Robbins' programs—which made it easy as we spoke the same language—but he also had very unique ideas about using video and technology to reach new customers and automate distribution of products in a compelling way. Most important, he's a person who predicates his success on the tangible *results* he's able to produce, not just on teaching or sharing theories about what he thinks might be possible.

Our biggest passion today is helping entrepreneurs take their vision and make it real, in a way that makes a difference for others in the process.

Making, marketing and launching products of your own is the fastest way we know to achieve the economic freedom you desire, and to create something meaningful that leverages your unique knowledge and experience.

I can't wait to hear the story of your success.

—Pam

When I was five years old, my dad gave me a real power jigsaw and full access to the "shop in the basement" that had lots of tools in it. My dad could fix just about anything and had a knack for figuring out how things work.

He passed that gift on to me - and as long as I can remember, I've been taking things apart, figuring out how they work and if time permitted, putting them back together!

I grew up in a lower middle-class environment - dad was (and still is at 75!) a barber with four kids, there weren't a lot of extras to go around. We grew up eating out of the garden and I made a lot of my own toys out of rubber bands, paper clips, string and blocks of wood.

I learned how to program computers when I was 14 and became a serial entrepreneur by 18 - mostly consulting, teaching people how to use and set up their computers and writing software for small business owners.

As long as I can remember, I've loved the idea of "personal development" and the "personal growth" business. As a kid, I devoured biographies about people who overcame incredible odds to achieve great things.

I really got introduced to the world of personal development after going through a painful divorce. I was broke, overweight, felt like a horrible failure, and was spiritually empty. That's when I discovered and started reading Deepak Chopra, Wayne Dyer and Tony Robbins books and listening to their audio cassettes.

During that painful time, my business was failing, I was nearly $250,000 in debt, paying my credit card bills with credit card checks and buying food on gas cards. With all my knowledge, know-how, creativity and entrepreneurial skills, why couldn't I succeed?

I was saved by a conversation with a good friend who suggested I go to a Tony Robbins event. My ticket was secured by a brand-new credit card a foolish company sent to me. Days later, I was on the phone with a Tony Robbins sales representative named Chris Hendrickson who signed me up for "Life Mastery".

Armed with a dream, a lot of pain and a desire to get my life in order, I found myself in a room filled with adults jumping up and down, screaming and hugging each other. To say I felt weird and out of place was an understatement. In Eagle Lake, Minnesota where I'm from, guys who hugged were gay.

But after a couple of days of watching, I decided to start smiling, jumping up and down and hugging guys because I had a "breakthrough". 90 days after leaving that live event, I turned most of my life around and less than a year later, my previously failing company was being purchased by a billion-dollar advertising agency.

Over the course of the next couple years, I studied online "direct response marketing" and started creating products, audio programs, video training and web sites for authors, experts, speakers, coaches and consultants.

And in 2004, I "became the star" and launched my own products online and started several online companies that earned millions of dollars over the next few years.

During this time, I had moved to San Diego (home of Tony Robbins), connected with my Tony Robbins sales rep, Chris Hendrickson, met his beautiful, kind and brilliant wife, Pam and we became fast friends (along with my wife, Vivian).

For years, Pam was Tony's "Product Development Specialist" - which meant if a product came out of that organization, Pam had her hand in making it. Pam eventually introduced me to Tony and I helped him and his company with a variety of online, video marketing, product creation and have even had the fortune of speaking at his live events.

I felt Tony's work saved my life. Now it was my turn to help him.

A couple years ago, I suggested that Pam, Chris and I start a business, combine our skills and create a business and products devoted to teaching small business owners, entrepreneurs, authors, experts, speakers, consultants and coaches how to make their own product and start self-sustaining, successful businesses of their own.

That was the start of "Make, Market, Launch IT" - and using the same skills we've spent over 40 years (combined) honing, we launched a business that earned over a million dollars in our first year.

This book and the product represent our experience and knowledge - and an opportunity to do the same for yourself, no matter what your knowledge, background or expertise is. No matter where in the world you live.

You can turn your knowledge into products that will change and improve lives and businesses, while making you wealthy in the process.

If you have an idea or think you could have an idea that can be turned into a product, you've found the right book, the right resources and the right people to help you on your journey.

Welcome to Make, Market, Launch IT!

— Mike

Introduction

We need more creators—and we need them now, more than ever.

We're in the Age of Information Overload. When computers first started appearing in homes, we measured data in kilobytes and megabytes. Now we measure it in exabytes—units of a *million* gigabytes each. In 2007, the amount of data available in the world was estimated as 297 exabytes. Stacked on discs, that's enough to reach past the moon into space.[1]

A staggering amount of that data is easily available to us with an Internet connection and a search engine. Eight *years* of content are uploaded to YouTube every day.[2] The entire history of the *New York Times*—13 million articles, starting from 1851—is available to search on their website.[3] 2.7 billion photos are available on Flickr alone.[4] We also share 1 billion items on Facebook every day.[5] And we're increasingly accessing this data in new ways, with almost 13% of Internet traffic coming from mobile devices.[6]

---

1   http://www.bbc.co.uk/news/technology-12419672
2   http://www.youtube.com/t/faq
3   http://www.nytimes.com/ref/membercenter/nytarchive.html
4   http://www.flickr.com/photos/franckmichel/6855169886/
5   http://news.cnet.com/8301-1023_3-57481153-93/facebook-1-billion-things-shared-via-open-graph-daily/
6   Embedded in: http://venturebeat.com/2012/12/03/mary-meeker-releases-stunning-data-on-the-state-of-the-internet/

But have you looked carefully at your search results lately? More and more, it's less about finding a source for your answers, and more about sifting through junk to find a credible source. It's also tougher to find resources with real meat to them. Many of the results are simply repeats of the same thin article, copied across 20 different websites. And still more are clearly generated by a robot who barely makes any sense.

In other words, there's a serious lack of quality out there, of real, credible, authentic human sources who have something meaningful to share.

That's where the sweet spot lies—and your opportunity.

If you've picked up this book, you likely have some kind of expertise at your disposal that you're looking to leverage.

Our research has shown that you've probably spent a significant amount of time in your field, honing your knowledge and skills. You've assembled an incredible wealth of knowledge from varied sources, including your education, your research and your experience in the field, all hard-earned.

Maybe you've spent fewer years in your field. But despite having less experience, you've made rapid progress through new distinctions that you're eager to reveal to others.

You might also be pursuing a slightly different track. Or, maybe you know someone else who has the potential to impact the world in a significant way, if only they could package their expertise so others can access it.

Regardless of your background, you have something to share: a unique perspective, a "take" on how the world works. And you're burning to share it. You deserve a chance to take all of that hard work, knowledge and experience and create something from which the rest of us can benefit.

In fact, we're clamoring to hear it. Amidst all the noise and the junk, you'll find listeners eager to enjoy the insights of an authentic, credible voice in the marketplace, offering hope and insight, as well as a path to change.

You deserve to share your message with the world, to impact people thousands of miles away who can use your distinctions as much as your next-door neighbor. It's your right to share your expertise and get your ideas heard now—and into the future. There's never been a better time to share your legacy.

There's also never been a better time to profit from it.

The Internet not only makes it possible, but also infinitely easier to share your message with the nearly 2.5 billion people who use the Internet around the world with their laptop and desktop computers[7] and the over 1 billion who are connected with a mobile device like a phone, smartphone or tablet.[8] With that kind of potential audience, you have the opportunity to earn an income of geometric proportions, one that will open your products to the world and free you from directly trading your time for money.

After all the work you've done, it's time for you to make the most of this opportunity. Maximize your existing product's earning potential or create a product based on your area of expertise. Then, build a real business around it, one that provides you with a consistent, healthy source of revenue, one that will free up your time so you can focus on what you love.

The door is open for you to start a Make, Market, Launch IT business.

Whatever your expertise, you can use Make, Market, Launch IT to support your goals and dreams at the highest level. All you have to do is put the stake in the ground for your vision. We'll show you how to build a business that will provide the means to make it a reality.

A Make, Market, Launch IT business will also help you serve your clients at the highest level. You'll create raving fan customers devoted to you and your mission. When you create products for them, you'll have a direct line to their innermost fears and joys, providing you the means to help them get to the heart of their challenges and solve them on their own terms. And when they reach one level, your Make, Market, Launch IT

---

7   http://www.internetworldstats.com/stats.htm
8   http://www.cbsnews.com/8301-205_162-57534583/study-number-of-smartphone-users-tops-1-billion/

portfolio will grow with them, creating innovative solutions at escalating levels. This creates both a continuous relationship with your customers and a source of consistent revenue.

As you create a full suite of products to meet your customers' changing needs, you'll continue with them on their journey of transformation.

Automating your marketing and delivery systems will enable you to create constant and consistent streams of revenue to sustain a thriving business with minimal day-to-day involvement on your part.

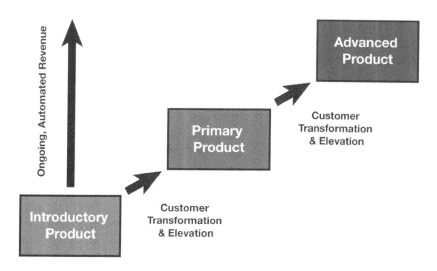

It's all possible with a Make, Market, Launch IT business and the process starts in this book.

In the next seven chapters, we'll show you how can you get your products to market quickly and inexpensively—while retaining the highest quality possible—so you can make an impact in your marketplace and start building a consistent revenue stream now.

It starts with a product, but the result is so much greater: a path of constant improvement for your clients and a real, revenue-generating business for you, one that empowers you to finally get paid for what you know.

The opportunity is here and it's real. It's yours for the taking. The world is full of potential customers who need your knowledge and experience. They need your voice, backed by your credibility.

And they need you now, more than ever.

As you establish your business, you'll be forming a huge—and vital—part of the economy. Small businesses employ more than 50% of the U.S.'s private sector workers and produce 13 times more patents than large patent firms.[9] Entrepreneurs drive innovation and, with it, the world economy.

Imagine what it would be like to design your own life at the intersection of your hard-earned experience, your deepest desires for yourself and the passion that gives your life excitement. Where is that intersection for you? Can you see yourself in that spot? What are you doing? What are you creating? It's something we'll help you continue to explore throughout this book.

In that intersection, you'll also find a group of people: your future clients. How are you going to use your unique perspective to help them? Where's the pain in their lives? Where's the pleasure? How can you help them get from one place to the other?

In other words, what problem can you solve for them to help improve their lives? How will you leave them in a better place by catalyzing change?

In that transformation, you'll find the heart of your first (or next) product. That's where you'll begin your journey. At the end, both you and your clients will be irrevocably changed for the better.

The rise of the Internet has created a singularly unique opportunity. Anyone with a laptop can have a voice, one that has the potential to be heard by billions of people across the world.

---

9 http://www.ritholtz.com/blog/2012/01/small-business-successfailure-rates/

And when you can combine that unparalleled access with something more—your unique cocktail of who you are, what you've seen, what you've done—**your voice will stand out as someone who needs to be heard.** You'll become someone we're dying to listen to, a welcome voice among all the static.

Your message and your legacy are waiting, along with your clients. It's time for your voice to be heard.

We'll be waiting, too. It's our personal mission to show people who've worked all their lives to become experts how to become successful entrepreneurs. We can't wait to see what you come up with.

How to Use This Book

As you start this journey, you may find it helpful to get a notebook to capture your ideas. It's one of the joys of the creative process that inspiration seems to strike while you're in line at Starbucks. Create a method to capture these thoughts—whether analog or digital. This will make sure that you benefit from your ideas before they get away.

You may be reading this book on your computer, your phone, your eReader, your iPad or you may be holding it in your hands. As you experience this message, we'll ask you at various points to complete an exercise to put a stake in the ground, generate some ideas or set some milestones for yourself.

We encourage you to capture your answers to these questions as you read. They'll help you shape your ideas as you move through the book and continue your momentum to support your Make, Market, Launch IT business as it takes flight.

As we dive in, we'd like to introduce you to one of the eight people you'll meet in this book who have used the Make, Market, Launch IT system to produce results. They'll show you how they turned their expertise, education and passion into a product that's changing lives. As you read these reports from the field, we hope they inspire you to take action and seize this remarkable opportunity.

We'll start with Sue Ferreira, a woman who turned an unexpected life change into her life's mission.

"This isn't work."
Case Study from the Field: Sue Ferreira, M.D.

As a successful physician for over 40 years and the mother of three, Sue Ferreira thought she had the rest of her life pretty much figured out. However, life threw her a curve ball when her marriage of 34 years ended and her "grey divorce" forced her to reassess her life.

Sue's first realization was how little she knew about managing her own finances. She immersed herself in books, websites—anything she could get her hands on—to craft a successful financial future, which would lead her to peace of mind in her later years. "I followed my nose, read widely and basically undertook a lay person's MBA," she says. "Initially, I was learning for myself, but eventually world events made me realize I had much to offer to others."

When the market crashed in 2008, Sue was struck with her mobilizing realization. Even before the crash, many knew they had inadequate savings to last their retirement years, and the downturn had accelerated those numbers. Millions would soon be in the same place she had been: forced to rebuild during their later years with limited time available. At that point, Sue realized she had a library of valuable knowledge on her hands. She had learned the hard way how to rebuild her life, both financially and emotionally, and knew she could fast track others and expedite the process. What could have been interpreted as disaster, Sue turned into an asset and an opportunity.

This shift in mindset was the beginning of a new life chapter for Sue. "I learned so much about building a new life myself, I knew I could create a holistic program that would allow people to work out how they could generate added income and live a successful financially secure retirement," she says.

Sue named her first product *Boomer-Bucks*, but struggled to get it off the ground. Without having much marketing experience, she didn't know how to take the product to the next level. "I was spinning my wheels," she says. "I looked at Mike and Pam's programs and decided I needed their experience to accelerate the process and get myself out there. I remember taking a big deep breath and saying to myself, 'Here I go!'"

"The structure of Make, Market, Launch IT is so logical and clear. If you just follow everything online or you follow the DVDs, you've got an absolutely beautiful algorithm of how to develop a product," she continues.

One of the biggest changes in Sue's mindset came after Make, Market, Launch IT strategies made her start thinking like a marketer, rather than, as she says, a "didactic teacher." She made the move from a decades-old, entrenched university style of teaching to coaching from a new perspective.

Sue redefined her target audience and renamed her program. "I learned to turn everything around and say to myself "I am my target market person right now. What do I want to receive from me?" Because of the way Pam changed the emphasis, now it's easy to see the process, and my progress has accelerated rapidly," Sue explains.

 **The result was _Live Your Retirement Dream,_** a new brand that embodied both what Sue was doing herself and what she wanted for others.

"I'm my own avatar, and think that's why I feel so passionately about this. I know how to do this. I've gathered and organized so much information and know I can fast-track any individual faced with starting a new venture. Many people have given up the idea of living their retirement dream, but giving up won't get you there and it just isn't an option, if you truly want to live your retirement dream." she continues.

To reach her audience and make money to show it can be done, Sue also realized she couldn't play small. "If you want to make a difference and you think about the millions of websites out there, they are all waving little flags trying to get your attention. You're just not going to be seen unless you do something different from everybody else," she says. "You have to be prepared to go out and absolutely make yourself be seen everywhere."

Make, Market, Launch IT showed her how to make that happen. "No one can do this on their own. I spent a lot of time looking at different experts before I found Pam and Mike and knew they were the ones I needed. They have more than the knowledge. They have mindset and the kind of heart and commitment that I want to associate myself with in order to succeed."

Sue released her book, *Live Your Retirement Dream*, in October 2012. "If I hadn't found Pam and Mike, I'd still be paddling around in the shallow end and wouldn't have jumped into the deep end and started swimming," she says. "Make, Market, Launch IT is an excellent product. Anybody who wants to develop a product, be effective, and market it well needs to buy this. It's a no-brainer. It's a savings, not an expense."

In the end, Sue's divorce and her subsequent life changes transformed her for the better. "I truly feel reborn. Apart from my kids, my divorce was the best thing that ever happened to me, because it allowed me to reassess my life and move into this new world, which I absolutely love. And, I assure you, if I can do it, anyone can."

Sue's advice for those wanting to follow in her footsteps? Play at a higher level. "You have to do it very well. If you don't do it very well, nobody is going to look at you. I made a lot of mistakes because I tried to do it all myself. If I had known about Mike and Pam and their programs four years ago, I'd be so much further ahead than I am now."

Thanks to Make, Market, Launch IT, Sue also has the strategies and the confidence to help her own clients make the most of their time: "I can take people from zero knowledge and show them how to fast track to their goals, without any wandering around and feeling lost and confused. I know how to get them off the deep end, now."

Ultimately, Sue couldn't be happier about where her Make, Market, Launch IT journey has led her. "I find it very exciting. I mean, this isn't work because I'm enjoying it so much."

Sue Ferreira's *Live Your Retirement Dream* is available on Amazon. com. She will launch her online course in mid-2013 at **www. LiveYourRetirementDream.com**.

"The great use of life is to spend it for
something that outlasts it."

—William James

Step 1: Mindset
Set Yourself Up for Success

Your product creation journey starts here, and we're so glad to have you with us.

This journey is about more than just an idea for a product—or even an amazing product by itself. This journey is about setting yourself up for what you want for yourself,—personally and professionally. Where do you want to be in the next five or ten years? How will you share your unique perspective with the world? Where does that perspective intersect with your passion? How do you want to spend your time? Where do you want to go? Who do you want to be? What do you want to create? What's your vision for your future?

And perhaps most importantly: How will building a business around your ideas and your products help you get there?

Achieving your vision starts with your mindset. Before you start generating ideas, drafting outlines or assembling prototypes, you need to put yourself in the right frame of mind to understand the pieces that will get you where you want to be. You need to find where your heart's desire intersects with your hard-earned knowledge.

In this chapter, we'll help you get really clear about what you want and how creating a product—and a real business with real revenue—can help you get there.

If your focus is on helping other people make, market and launch their products, this chapter will also show you how to help your clients get clear on what they want from their businesses. So many business owners have forgotten their original goals. If you can help them reassociate to their original intent—and the excitement that surrounds their vision, purpose, drive and reason for doing what they do—you'll add tremendous value and be paid well for it, too.

The product creation mindset is ultimately about three things:

1. Destination
2. Momentum
3. Progress

Three simple things, really. But three powerful fulcrums that will give you the strong foundation you need to create products that excite you, products that improve other peoples' lives. And then, on that foundation, we'll show you how to build your legacy and live a sustainable, enjoyable lifestyle—the lifestyle of your dreams.

But, it starts with the right mindset. We'll begin by examining the thought process of the best of the best: the millionaire entrepreneur.

Seven Traits of the Millionaire Entrepreneur

The most successful entrepreneurs—regardless of background, age, sex, credentials or experience—understand that effective business-building strategies are only part of the equation. They recognize that most of their results come from an empowered psychology that allows them to follow through and apply the strategies that create growth.

After consulting with the best of the best—entrepreneurs, authors, celebrities and CEOs like Tony Robbins; John Assaraf from "The Secret"; Darren Hardy, creator of *SUCCESS* magazine; and brand experts Simon Mainwaring and Brian Tracy; business development leaders Ken

Blanchard, Tim Ferriss, Frank Kern and Harvey Mackay; and hundreds more—we've observed the following seven common character traits. Which of these do you posess?

1. **They have incredibly high standards—for themselves, their product, their customer service, their staff and their customers.** They often believe more in their customers than their customers believe in themselves. Standards aren't created when things are going well. They show up when times are tough, when you're confronted with things you don't necessarily want to do. Standards are created to serve the higher interests of your business and your customers, in good times and challenging times.

2. **They are focused first and foremost on the customer.** The most successful entrepreneurs got into their business because they really care about people, not their own egos. They're driven by a strong desire to empower others to create the lives they truly want. They care more about their customers than they do about their actual products and services.

3. **They're committed to continued education.** The people who get ahead are like sponges, soaking up all the distinctions they can. They never stop learning and constantly feed their minds with quality information, both about their field and others as well.

4. **They employ a "Zero Negativity Policy."** Go-getters simply don't tolerate bad days, negative thoughts or negative behaviors that do not support the business, their "big why" or their vision. That's not to say everything is perfect, but when something inevitably goes awry, they don't live there. They shift their focus, and help their colleagues and staff members do the same.

5. **They have a powerful vision and clarity of purpose.** Leaders maintain their vision in the face of the challenges they experience along the way. Their vision excites and inspires those around them to be part of it. They cultivate an attitude of abundance, allowing them to see opportunities when they appear.

6. **They've experienced several real failures on their road to success.** Success isn't measured by the absence of failures. It's measured by the ability to take those failures and learn from them to produce better results in the future—and to continue to act, even when things get tough. This requires both the honesty to recognize failures and the ability to continue to take calculated risks, despite past challenges. Both will foster future success.

7. **They recognize that with their success comes a responsibility to give back, both with time and money and by empowering others to improve the quality of their lives.** They follow their words with actions and pay their success forward, with the interest in truly making the world a better place.

With the philosophies of the best of the best in mind, what's your ultimate vision for your future?

Destination • Momentum • Progress

The first step toward living your ultimate vision is understanding exactly what that means for you, in specific terms, down to the little actions and emotions that create meaning.

Let's look closely at the question we started with:

What's your ultimate vision for yourself?

Take the time to really think about the answer, even if you've done it before. Steal a few quiet minutes away from your email, away from your text messages, even away from your partner or your family and really *think*.

What do you want? Where do you envision yourself in six months? Five years? Ten years? What have you always dreamed of creating for yourself? How do you spend your days? Where do you put your energy? How do you renew it?

And why? What's behind that vision? What is your "big why?" Who's with you in that vision? What's driving you and motivating you to reach it? When you arrive at this destination, who will you be? How will you feel?

Really dig into that vision. If you dream of retiring to a small Caribbean island, feel the sand between your toes. If you imagine headlining a live event, picture yourself on stage in front of thousands of people, with huge screens displaying your product. If you picture more time with your kids, watch them kicking a soccer ball back to you.

What's your ultimate vision for yourself? And why? Describe it, using all the details and emotions you feel.

There is immense power in these images.

This vision—and the emotions that come along with them—are your motivation. They're the things that wake you with a stir of anticipation in the morning. They're the Energizer in your bunny that will keep you going, day after day, when things are going swimmingly and when times are tough. When you get fully associated with the emotions you will experience when you achieve your vision and your goals, hitting your target becomes that much easier.

"Destiny is no matter of chance. It is a matter of choice. It is not a thing to be waited for, it is a thing to be achieved."

—William Jennings Bryan

Put your vision in a place where you can come back to it, time and time again, when you need a boost. Your vision is the fuel that ignites the passion and hunger that will turn it into reality.

How Will Creating Your Product Help You Get There?

That's what we're here to help you discover. It starts with you and the reason you're here: your unique perspective that you have to offer the world. It's been shaped by your education, whether from a university or the school of hard knocks, your years of experience, and the time and energy you've put into honing your expertise. It's fueled by your passion and your drive, and it's entirely, uniquely yours.

When you combine all of these things into a product that other people can enjoy, you'll be able to:

1. **Leverage Your Time:** If you find yourself showing people how to do the same things repeatedly, it's time to create a product that teaches these lessons without you there. This will allow you to put your focus and energy on the things you are most excited about—and the things that grow your business. Most importantly, you will be able to sell your product instead of your time—and charge more for your time if and when you choose to sell it.

2. **Monetize Your Expertise:** Until you have a product that leverages your time, you will always be trading your time for money. When you're in the position of a 1:1 trade, you'll find it incredibly difficult to scale your income and create lasting wealth. By developing products that can be applied without your presence, you will put yourself in the position to make money while you sleep—and exponentially grow your income. Once you have this single puzzle piece in place, your income and momentum will start to build quickly. New opportunities will appear—such as licensing your content, product endorsements, television and speaking opportunties and much more—raising your visibility and your credibility to an even higher level.

3. **Make Yourself Competition-Proof:** Nobody else has your unique life experience or knowledge. When you are properly positioned in your market with a product to sell, you automatically gain trust and authority. This unique combination makes you competition-proof. Your perspective and message will have more value than another person or company simply because you're more visible.

Is Mehmet Oz the most knowledgeable doctor in the world? How about Deepak Chopra? Dr. Phil? What about someone like Suze Orman? Is she the smartest financial guru there is? Is Anthony Bourdain the savviest food guy there is? No. It's their story, their visibility, their fame and connections that make them more valuable. Every one of them started out with no fame, trust, authority or visibility. They didn't "get" lucky. They created their brands, reinforced their expertises by packaging them into a "product" they could sell—a book, a television show, an audio program—and *made* their luck.

4. **Build Your Legacy:** When you create products and services for your marketplace, they can be consumed by anyone in the world, anywhere and at any time. Instead of training one-on-one or at a live event setting, you can put yourself in a position to impact more lives without the potential barriers of time or travel. Creating a product allows you to build a legacy beyond what you are able to physically do as an individual.

As you create your product, keep this principle top of mind:

The ultimate goal of any business—or product—is to produce outstanding, ongoing results for customers.

In other words, if you only focus on doing these two things, you can be successful:

1. Adding value

2. Creating customer success

Building a business of this nature places abundance at its core. If you're giving authentically, from the heart, that will attract customers and the power of transformation will naturally take over.

Six Magic Questions of Success

Ask yourself the following questions to sharpen your vision for the product you'd like to develop. Give yourself a clear target for continuing on this journey. If you plan to help others create products and services, you can use this set of questions both to shape your vision for your consulting business as well as to help your clients shape their product ideas. And, if you'd like to maximize an existing product, these questions will help you define the next level you are seeking.

6 Magic Questions:

1. **What product are you committed to make now?** When will you launch it?

2. **Who are you going to sell it to?** Who are you committed to serve with your product or service? What pain does it alleviate? What problem does it cure?

3. **How much will you charge for your product?** Go with your gut and keep in mind that we'll refine this in Step 3. If you're uncertain, take a look at your competitor's products, or ask yourself how much someone would pay a professional or consultant to cure the problem.

4. **What is your goal for how much money you want to make with this product or service in the first 12 months?**

5. **How many products do you need to sell to achieve this?**

6. **Why is this important to you?** What will you do—and who will you help—with this money?

The Cycle of Transformation

As you continue to help new customers transform, success stories will beging to emerge. Each one has the potential to spread like wildfire and bring new customers. They also create repeat customers. When you shift your focus toward who you can serve, it's a win all around.

Because our goal is to help you build a *business*, we want you to focus on *ongoing* transformation—on serving your clients at multiple levels. Think about helping them continually escalate their results through a suite of products.

We call it a Client Path, a system of creating complementary products that help your clients continue to make progress and create change at varying levels.

Can you imagine a customer experiencing that kind of lifelong transformation? It's one of the greatest gifts you can offer someone— and one of the most rewarding.

The Cycle of Transformation

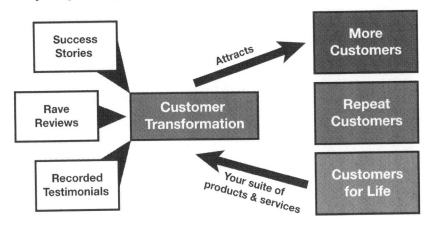

Building Your Client Path

Putting together a suite of escalating products starts with this core idea:

What do your customers need at each stage of the game in order to get to the next level?

You can think about it in three phases.

The Three Levels of Product Offerings:

1. **Introductory Products:** Free or low-price content with high value directed to engage your target market.

2. **Primary Products:** Main products or services (i.e. what you're known for), usually organized into a step-by-step training system.

3. **Advanced Products:** High-end, more customized products or services, usually based on high-touch, high personalization.

At each step, you're solving a specific piece of your customer's problem. You're meeting your clients where they are and taking them to where they want to be. That's when the magic happens.

What's Your Escalation Plan?

At this point in your journey, you may already have a finished product, you may have a work in progress or you may be starting this journey from scratch. Regardless of where you are at right now, you should know the problem you are solving for your clients.

So, where do you go from here? Once a client or customer uses your product and achieves their desired result, they'll naturally ask: "What else do you have?" It's at this point that you have the opportunity to solve additional problems or challenges through programs of advanced complexity, which are worth a higher price point.

That's escalation—rising to the next level. An escalation plan is a natural progression from your first to your second, third, fourth or fifth products.

There's escalation built into every successful business. For example, let's look at the automotive industry. A college student might start out with a Toyota Corolla. As he gets his first big job, he gets a Camry. Then, once he gets promoted, he may move on to the luxury Toyota brand: the Lexus.

How will you build your escalation plan? Consider the problem you want to solve for your customers and look at the three phases below. Where does it fall?

The Client Problem Cycle:

Fill in the problem you are solving in the blank chart below. Now look at the other two blank areas. What problem can you solve in the other two parts of the cycle?

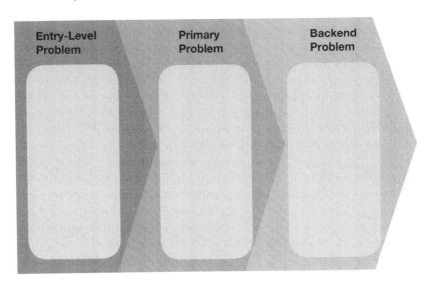

Entry-Level Problem   Primary Problem   Backend Problem

Destination • **Momentum** • Progress

Now that you've generated some ideas for what you want for yourself and what you plan to create, it's time to set up the habits that will make these ideas reality.

Momentum is about the reality of how things get done: small, consistent actions over days and weeks.

Take regular forward-moving actions toward your goal no matter what, and you'll create the momentum to get there.

You might think of it like running a race by putting one foot in front of the other, with no regard for the other runners, the time ticking away or the distance to the finish line. If you follow the path you created—if you aim toward your destination—you'll get there.

Looking in the Mirror:

Maintaining forward motion also requires acknowledging yourself.

Look within and ask:

1. Is there something that's been holding me back?
2. What's been keeping me from taking my life—and my business—to the next level?
3. What kinds of tasks do I distract myself with that keep me from achieving my true goal?

Now ask yourself: What's the cure? Better yet, what are the new habits you can put in place to keep yourself from reverting back?

What will you do to eliminate what's holding you back? How will you remove any final barriers to creating momentum?

 ## Greater Focus, Greater Effectiveness:
The Pomodoro Technique

If your challenge lies in getting things done, you might want to check out the Pomodoro Technique. This time- and mind-management system is built on breaking your productive time into 25-minute chunks, separated by breaks. These short bursts of productivity boost your output, while building in time to let your brain recharge for increased stamina. The system also includes additional principles for optimizing your time. It's perfect for entrepreneurs who are trying to make the most out of a tight schedule.

Read more about the Pomodoro Technique at **PomodoroTechnique.com**.

One More Note

Before we move on, we want to take a quick break to say one more thing. In these exercises—and in any steps you take toward your Make, Market, Launch IT goals—remember this:

Perfection is not your goal.

Whoever first said "Perfection is the enemy of progress" was, in our minds, a genius.

Take it from us: you'll never love your first product. The product creation process is so transformative that the progress you make in a week will suddenly make you re-think the video you shot last Tuesday.

It's natural. It's good.

There's a time to go back and reshoot the video and there's a time to decide that it's good enough for the time being. Only you can draw that line. It's a tough call, for sure. One of the toughest you'll ever make.

Here's what we can tell you. If you constantly choose the first option—and keep re-shooting, rewriting and redesigning—you'll never launch a product. At some point, you have to put your foot down, stop fixing and move forward.

However, you can remember to honor yourself for the action you've taken. Your first product may not be perfect, but it's your first stake in the ground. There's beauty in that.

It also represents one of the most precious things in the product creation process: progress.

Destination • Momentum • **Progress**

Progress is what happens when your little steps begin to add up to something greater. It's also something that should be celebrated.

As you manage your psychology throughout this process, we suggest you do two things:

1. Celebrate each step of progress you make, no matter how small.

2. Break absolutely everything down into manageable chunks that you can easily tackle.

Doing these two things will ensure that you enjoy your accomplishments as you build a successful business.

Dealing with Speed Bumps

After each being in this business for 20+ years, we know firsthand: stuff happens. Even creators with the best mindsets can get rattled. Here's what we suggest to help you deal with challenges along the way and stay on track.

1. **Plan for it.** Expecting things to go wrong isn't pessimistic. It's realistic. If you expect the unexpected, you'll have an easier time reacting well to it.

2. **Reassociate yourself to your big why.** If things get tough, go back to the reason you're doing this in the first place: financial freedom, more time with family, flexibility in your schedule or whatever you associate with the most emotion. Those feelings will help you get back on track ASAP.

3. **Keep a reminder handy.** For times when inspiration is tough to come by, post a picture near your workspace of something that reminds you of your goal. Whether or not you consciously look at it, it will serve as a constant unconscious reminder of the motivation behind your actions.

4. **Reach out.** We're grateful to have each other when the going gets tough. Being an entrepreneur can get lonely, so make sure you establish a network of trusted friends and colleagues who can talk you through any challenges.

5. **Associate to the *who*.** When challenges arise, it helps to think about who you're doing this for: your customers. We suggest keeping your customer top-of-mind as you create your product. This single, simple distinction will not only give you direction but will inspire a contribution-focused mindset. It will keep your intentions pure and keep you connected to your deeper purpose. Both of us feel the product creation process is a spiritual exercise! Staying connected to the greater purpose will help you keep the faith.

6. **Just get started.** The infamous (and now deceased) copywriter, Gary Halbert, invented the "blah, blah, blah" technique. If you've come down with a case of writers' block, just sit down and start typing (or writing). If you don't have anything to say, just start typing "blah, blah, blah." The forward momentum you build will put your body in motion. Your creative mind will follow and quickly take over.

It might sound crazy, but it works. Some of the greatest writers whoever lived wrote a minimum of a page a day. At the end of a year, that's 365 pages. How many years of your life have passed without writing a single book?

It's All About You

Your mindset—your approach and the strategies that support it—can't be underestimated. They're the foundation of a business, especially one that's built on you and your expertise.

That's why we started your product creation journey here: to emphasize its importance.

Your mindset will set you up for success. You have the tools and strategies needed to mentally get yourself to the place you need to be.

So... 1) take stock and 2) make a commitment. It's time to identify your target audience.

But first, we'd like you to meet another one of our success stories, Ila Scott-Ford. Ila used the mindset strategies in Make, Market, Launch IT to do what she hadn't been able to do previously: turn her idea into a living, breathing product.

"I'm nearly ready to launch."
Case Study from the Field: Ila Scott-Ford

An inventor by spirit and a Chief Marketing Officer by trade, product ideas come naturally to Ila Scott-Ford. During an evening walk in 2005, Ila came up with an idea that she believed filled a huge unmet need. The key to its success would be creating the ideal brand name, one with the potential to become a household name.

The result of that late-night idea, *Let Family Know*™, is a suite of products designed to make it easy to create the important information you'd want family and friends to know, if anything should happen to you.

So often death or a debilitating accident or illness comes as a surprise. Families are left panicked and frustrated trying to find information, and often hard feelings are generated over the decisions that get made. Ila saw the opportunity for a simple, inexpensive, straightforward way to share vital personal and financial information. "I saw Let Family Know products as something I could create to serve others and get meaning out of what I do. It's my true life's purpose, my calling," she says.

After shaping the idea, Ila began work developing her brand. She took an eight-week entrepreneur class at the University of Iowa, wrote a business plan and began working on a series of products with a corresponding website. However, with a fast-paced job as an advertising executive, progress didn't happen fast enough.

Everything changed when she discovered Make, Market, Launch IT. "The whole Make, Market, Launch IT experience changed everything for me. It gave me a sense of not only the 'hows' of product creation, but also the 'whys' and the 'ways,'" she explains.

"I knew without a doubt that this course is what I needed to make something happen," she says.

"[It] was the catalyst I needed to give me direction and break the big process of product creation into manageable sized steps so I could see the path for creating even more products," she continues.

This new injection of direction gave her the fuel she needed to set forth on a results-driven path. By breaking the process down into doable-sized, step-by-step chunks, Ila feels confident that her product line will continue to grow and develop.

Make, Market, Launch IT also helped Ila remove several roadblocks during the creation process.

As she was a one-person company, Ila felt like she was living an "isolated and time-starved life." Make, Market, Launch IT connected her to a network of people with bigger ideas, which helped to draw her out and renew her excitement for her project.

The demands of her full-time job also made it easy to put her product on the back burner. The Make, Market, Launch IT structure, including the weekly training webinars, helped her stay on course. "I love that I can go back to the MML site 24/7 to revisit the strategies. The content is so well organized that it's easy to find the exact coaching I need."

Ila also credits the Module 1 advice to "get [her product] out there" without trying to "make it perfect" on the first release as helping her make significant progress.

Finally, Ila shares that she has a fear of overwhelm—"getting in over her head"—which often sidetracked her previous efforts. However, by following the steps within the product and tackling them one at a time, Ila is making great strides in finally getting *Let Family Know* off the ground and into the hands of the consumers who need it.

"Even with 27 years of marketing experience under my belt, Make, Market, Launch IT took me to another level. [It] brought me up to date with today's digital and online marketing strategies and gave me the tools and connections to make anything happen so I can get my products out and start helping people," she explains.

After seven years of brainstorming, Ila is finally about to bring her product to life, in a fraction of the time.

"Without Make, Market, Launch IT, I wouldn't be as far along as I am. I'm nearly ready to launch."

Ila Scott-Ford's *Let Family Know* launches in 2013 at **LetFamilyKnow.com**.

Step 2: Target
Identify & Connect with Your Ideal Market

Creating a real business out of your idea requires a core group of people to support it: *customers* to buy what you have to sell.

And yet, when many people sit down to create their product, they don't know exactly who they're going to sell it to. They might have a general understanding that their product will appeal to a general audience such as moms looking to lose a few pounds or business owners looking to sharpen their sales techniques.

Because we want to help you create a product that prospects line up to buy, we want you to get more specific. You can't build a full suite of successful products without a specific and clearly defined audience. When you create your product, make it with real people in mind. Know your ideal customer and *everything* about them—their age, sex, names, kids' names, biggest challenges, their dreams, aspirations, fears, psychological wounds, and more. We call this overview of your ideal client, *an avatar.*

You need particulars on who your customers will be, in full and vivid detail. If possible, it will be even better to know *names* of the actual people who fit this profile.

When we surveyed a group of entrepreneurs who were in the early phases of their product creation business, only 6% of them had more than 500 contacts on their marketing list. More than half of them didn't have a list at all, perhaps because they didn't yet have the tools, time or strategies to get out there and find potential clients. And yet nearly half of them had already created a product.

Keep in mind that these numbers represent the people with high awareness in the field, who recognized their need clearly enough to invest in it.

Spending the time to understand conceptually and realistically who you're going to sell your product to—BEFORE you start creating it is what will set you apart in your market.

Let's look at why.

In the last chapter, we gave you two guiding principles that will make you successful in your product creation business:

1. Add value
2. Create customer success

If you don't understand *who* you're doing this for—or what they need—achieving these two things is impossible.

That's why we need to add one additional element:

1. Add value
2. Create customer success
3. …by targeting the right people.

And who are the "right" people? They're the people who you can help. The people who value your expertise, who will pay you for the solutions you can offer them.

If you pour a glass of water for a person who's just hiked across the desert, you'll be their new best friend. That glass of water simply doesn't have the same value to a person who's sitting next to a water fountain.

Successful marketers are always on the lookout for a wounded, starving crowd. Then they find a product or service to fill that void.

As product creators, we tend to get emotional about our products. The end result is that we hypnotize ourselves into believing we have a solution to our customer's problems. There are literally millions of unsuccessful creators—many with superior products—who failed because they never figured out how to effectively communicate with their market.

Here's a fantastic story from the late, great Gary Halbert about focusing on the market:

As you may or may not know, every once in a while I give a class on copywriting and/or selling by mail. During these classes, one of the questions I like to ask my students is: *"If you and I both owned a hamburger stand and we were in a contest to see who could sell the most hamburgers, what advantages would you most like to have on your side to help you win?"*

The answers vary. Some of the students say they would like to have the advantage of having superior meat from which to make their burgers. Others say they want sesame seed buns. Others mention location. Someone usually wants to be able to offer the lowest prices.

And so on.

In any case, after my students are finished telling me what advantages they would most like to have, I usually say to them something like this: *"O.K., I'll give you every single advantage you have asked for. I, myself, only want one advantage and, if you will give it to me, I will (when it comes to selling burgers) whip the pants off all of you!"*

"What advantage do you want?" they ask.

"The only advantage I want," I reply, *"... is...a starving crowd!"*

Think about it. When it comes to direct marketing, the most profitable habit you can cultivate is the habit of constantly being on the lookout for groups of people (markets) who have demonstrated that they are starving (or, at least *hungry*) for some particular product or service.

Why You Need to Get Clear

Before you start your creation process—before you put pen to paper, before you make a single sketch and before you even begin to browse for your dream domain name—you need to get 100% crystal clear on two things:

1. Who EXACTLY is going to buy what you're creating?
2. Why will they buy it?

This clarity will help you build a *business* around your idea in the following ways:

1. **Your Marketing Messages Will Write Themselves.** When you get your audience on a deeper level, you'll also be able to connect with them authentically—and easily. You'll understand what they need to hear and how you should deliver it. Writing sales copy or making a video will become easy, like writing a letter to your mom or a good friend. And the more real your message is, the more likely they are to buy from you because you feel authentic to them.

2. **You'll Attract More Customers to You.** The British grocery chain, Tesco, has made a habit of getting to know its customers and sending them carefully crafted offers to match their needs. Tesco's rewards club data revealed that new fathers buy more beer at the store, as opposed to drinking it at pubs with their friends. They mailed new families coupons for beer as well as diapers, resulting in 8-14% redemption rates, as opposed to the 1-2% usually seen by other stores.[10]

Understanding your customers' needs—especially the ones they don't articulate—will bring people to you in droves. You'll also be able to time your messages to when your prospects are more likely to buy from you.

---

10 http://hbr.org/2011/12/know-what-your-customers-want-before-they-do/ar/1

3. **You'll Command Premium Prices.** Think back to the example of our friend who crossed the desert. What if you could give that person more than a glass of water? What if you could offer her a specially formulated drink to 1) replace the electrolytes she'd lost during her journey that would 2) relieve her calf cramps from dehydration and 3) help her body recover for the marathon she's running next week? Wouldn't she pay more for that drink than she would for that glass of water? Absolutely—because you understand her specific needs and you're meeting her *where* she is, not where you guess she might be.

4. **You'll Lose That Icky "Selling" Feeling.** Pairing problems with their solutions is like being a matchmaker. It's easy. It's fun. There's no need to pressure someone or to put on the hard sell. If you don't like to sell, getting clear on your target market is the ticket. This is the difference between elegant salesmanship and pushing your product on anyone you can to meet your revenue goals. So many entrepreneurs, authors, experts, speakers, consultants and coaches say they "don't like to sell." Often, they're confusing "solving problems" with being "pushy." Feeling good about your product and solution and helping people solve problems is the heart of good salesmanship.

5. **You'll Create Change.** When you match up the right problem with the right solution, you'll deliver results. You'll change lives. Results create social proof and testimonials, which cycle back to more customers, more sales and customers for life.

So what happens when you don't get clear?

The Flip Side

You end up with a garage full of products and no one to sell them to.

The *New York Times* recently reported that self-published books sell fewer than 100-150 copies.[11]

---

11 http://www.nytimes.com/2012/08/16/technology/personaltech/ins-and-outs-of-publishing-your-book-via-the-web.html?pagewanted=all&_r=0

150 copies. Think about that. This is a heart-breaking statistic.

As it relates to your ideal customers, a garage full of products happens for three reasons:

1. **Your product isn't specific enough to add value or create success.** We've seen this hundreds (or probably thousands) of times. When we ask a new product creator or author: "Who's your target audience?" and he replies, "Everyone," we know there's a big problem. If you try to be everything to everybody, you'll end up reaching nobody. When you don't understand exactly who you're creating products for, you can't address their acute problems. You'll end up with a generic product that offers watered-down solutions, instead of aiming an arrow that right in the bull's-eye of your ideal client's issues. It's not worth top dollar—and it may not be worth anything at all.

2. **You might have a target market, but you won't know how to find them or how to reach them.** You may have created something of incredible value, but if you can't get it in front of anyone who cares, your products will sit gathering dust. One of the most powerful questions you can ask yourself is: "Who owns the minds and hearts of the prospect I'm trying to reach?" If you have a great product, know how to communicate with your perfect prospect AND know how to access them, you've struck gold. Success can be a phone call or email away.

3. **Your target market either isn't large enough, or it's just not willing to pay to solve its problems.** That's the power of investigating your target market before you start creating: you'll know the size of your niche and you'll know if they're willing to spend money to solve their problems. For you to hit it out of the park, both of these things have to be true.

If you've already got a garage full of products, the techniques in this chapter can still help you locate your target market.

You can also take comfort in the fact that you're not alone.

This phenomenon is part of small business reality. Take a look at this recent research regarding the top ten reasons why new businesses go under:[12]

---

10 Reasons for New Business Failures:

1. Lack of experience
2. Insufficient capital
3. Poor location
4. **Poor inventory management (which includes having too many products that no one wants)**
5. Over-investment in fixed assets
6. Poor credit arrangements
7. Personal use of business funds
8. Unexpected growth
9. **Competition**
10. **Low sales**

What do the three highlighted items all have in common?

They're all symptoms of a poorly defined market.

It's About Simplifying.

Identifying your target market is a process of whittling away who your target market *isn't* until all that remains are the perfect clients for you. It's about making things *easier*—by simplifying.

It's about recognizing that you can't be everything to everybody. Wouldn't you rather make a strong contribution to fewer people—and impact them more significantly?

---

12 See credits at the bottom of this image for source data: http://www.creditdonkey.com/image/1/small-business-sink-or-swim.png

The alternative, of course, is spreading yourself too thin and ultimately impacting nobody. We'd choose the former ten times out of ten.

Consider One Final Statistic: In their book, *The Breakthrough Imperative*, Mark Gottfredson and Steve Schaubert quote research showing that less complex companies grow 80–100% faster than the most complex companies.[13]

In other words: keep it simple.

Locate the people who appreciate what you have to offer—and are willing to invest in it. Add value to their lives and help them create success. It's what a strong foundation for your Make, Market, Launch IT business is built on.

When we say "avatar," we're not talking about blue aliens from the James Cameron film. Your avatar will represent the aggregate demographic and psychographic profile of a perfect customer. Once you have identified this person, creating your product and marketing will become much more predictable.

Example: Your Ideal Client Avatar

1. **Overall group:** *moms*

2. **Gender:** *female*

3. **Education:** *college (4-year, bachelor of arts degree)*

4. **Profession:** *stay-at-home mom*

5. **Income:** *$100,000/year*

6. **Geographic Location:** *Colorado, US*

7. **Family & Lifestyle:** *2 kids (4 & 6), one more on the way*

8. **Online Activity (where can you find this person):** *active on mom blogs and parenting websites, as well as Facebook and Pinterest*

9. **Authority or Trust Figures (what celebrities or authorities do they know, like and trust):** *Oprah, Anderson Cooper, Michelle Obama*

---

13 http://www.economist.com/node/12762429

10. **If she could snap her fingers and make 3 changes in her life happen immediately, what would they be?** *(1) She and her husband, Jake, would make more time for each other away from the kids (2) She would lose 10 pounds (3) She would take her whole family on vacation twice a year.*

11. **What is her single biggest fear?** *That she and her husband will become better roommates than partners.*

12. **What must your avatar believe about you and your product or service to buy from you?** *She must believe that you are trustworthy and that you'll treat her money with as much care as she does.*

Give this avatar a name: *Melissa*

Use these questions as a jumping-off point. If you're inspired to learn more about your avatar, go for it. The more time you can spend getting to know this person and what they really want and need, the better. Especially when we're creating high-end products, it's not unusual for us to spend several hours to a few weeks investigating our ideal client avatar from top to bottom.

Depending on your avatar, your research might begin in the "Online Activity" arena. We usually start with the big five—Google+, Twitter, Facebook, Pinterest, LinkedIn—and start poking around. To complete this level of research, we'll go to live events, network with potential customers and participate in online forums to understand who our clients are and how we can best serve them.

Regardless of how much time you spend, by the time you finish the mental picture of your avatar, you should know him or her like a close friend.

Cultivate that closeness. It will bring authenticity and warmth to everything you do—and allow you to continually attract the right clients to your business.

This is also how surveys can become invaluable for understanding your ideal clients' deepest desires.

In other words: seek, observe and communicate. You'll start to fill in the puzzle and discover everything you need to know.

Rounding Out the Picture

Once you get the hang of creating an avatar for your ideal client, we want you to do one more thing: understand who you *don't* want to attract. We call these people "nightmare clients." They're psychic vampires, ready to suck your energy, waste your time and cause all sorts of problems.

Why should you take the time to understand the people you *don't* want to serve? First of all, it may help you clarify your ideal clients by creating a study in contrast.

Also, there may be times in your business when you might think "any client is a good client." If you're in scarcity mode, this will ring true for you. It's those times, when you feel like you're on a long, lonely road with no clients in view for *miles*, that you might be willing to deposit any check that comes across your desk.

Trust us, it's not worth it.

Nightmare clients suck up your money and resources. They order your products (multiple times!) and return them each time, sometimes after the return window, accompanied by a sob story. Nightmare clients badger your customer service staff when their email doesn't get answered within 20 minutes. Nightmare clients will also bug you for "extras" that they think they deserve by virtue of being clients, like private meetings and personalized resources. For some reason, they believe they're entitled to more.

But here's the real bummer:

Your product will, unfortunately, not add value to the lives of nightmare clients.

And even if it does, they'll never recognize it.

No matter how hard you try, you won't be able to help these clients improve their lives because the product you've made simply isn't for them. And like vampires, once you invite them into your home, they're hard to uninvite. Don't let them in. You'll regret it.

Creating a visual image for your nightmare clients enables you to recognize these people from a distance. It allows you to run away before they even make contact, allowing you to save your marketing dollars, sales efforts and precious energy.

Remember, this process is about *simplifying*.

It's not about one-size-fits-all, come-one, come-all. It's about tailor-making a solution that fits the right people like a custom Italian suit jacket. Some people will find it too tight through the shoulders. *That's okay.* We hope, by now, that you can see why you should still continue to tailor your solutions.

Answer a few questions to help you clarify—and avoid—a potential nightmare:

1. What kind of qualities will be a barrier to success? For example, if you're creating a system to win at online poker, your clients can't be 100% risk averse.

2. What level of skill *won't* work? If you're hosting a live event to share advanced sales techniques, it might be too complicated for a newbie sales professional.

3. What kind of outlook or attitude would prove disastrous? If you've created a series of environmentally friendly cleaning products, they just won't appeal to someone who doesn't possess any desire to contribute to the greater good of the world.

4. What have your other nightmare clients looked like? If you've ever clashed with a customer, investigate the qualities that caused the disconnect. Once you recognize these, and any others above, you'll know what to avoid in the future.

The Next Step: Turning Avatars into Actual Living & Breathing Clients

We started this chapter by telling you that you need to get clear on two items:

1. Who EXACTLY is going to buy what you're creating?
2. Why will they buy it?

This chapter—and the avatar exercises within—will help you form a complete answer to question #1.

The answer to question #2 starts with the psychology motivating your avatar. In the next chapter, we'll complete this answer by showing you how to construct an offer they can't resist. We'll also discuss how to position your product in a way that's irresistible to your prospects. In other words, we'll show you how to turn your avatar into living, breathing clients.

But before you can package your idea in a way that sells, there's one more thing you need to consider: you.

The Foundation of Your Product: Credibility

To get where you're going, you need to maximize where you're from.

We're talking about your credibility, the particular expertise or point of view that you're sharing with the world by creating a product.

Credibility is what makes people trust you.

It's what makes people believe you when you say: "It works." Without credibility, you might sell a few products here and there to people willing to take a risk, but you'll never have a landslide day.

At the end of the day, credibility = conversion.

We've spent this chapter showing you how to connect deeply with your audience. Credibility is what will round out that connection and convince people that it's okay to open their wallets and buy from you.

So, how do you build credibility?

Some people believe that credibility comes exclusively from education or degrees. While these factors contribute to your expertise and experience, showing someone a degree from Harvard is probably not going to close a sale (unless, of course, you're selling a book on how to get into Harvard).

Past successes form a significant part of your credibility. That's why social proof in the form of testimonials is so powerful.

But credentials can also come from another place: your willingness to share yourself, your ability to be authentic and your commitment to serving others. This clearly isn't something that's built overnight, but there are some simple techniques that you can use to demonstrate your credibility to your audience without having to spend years getting to know them.

One of our favorites is called the **Fool-Proof Formula,** which is great to use during a presentation. We'll discuss presentations in greater detail in Chapter 3, but, for now, it's enough to understand the foundation:

1. It starts when you **Make a Promise**: "I am going to show you three ways to reconnect with your husband and increase your intimacy immediately."

2. Then, you **Deliver on the Promise** by sharing what you promised.

3. Afterward, you **Confirm the Delivery**: "These are three simple techniques for reconnecting with your husband. Try them out in the next few days. I know you'll see the effects immediately."

Even before Melissa tries these techniques on her husband, she'll already feel like she can trust you: you promised her something and you delivered. (And if you followed our process, it's likely you even over-delivered.)

This creates an immense amount of credibility for you in a very short period of time.

If that promise can deliver on the Holy Grail, what Internet marketer Frank Kern calls "results in advance," meaning that Melissa sees a change in her husband, your credibility explodes and, with it, your conversions.

Now that you understand the power of defining your market, we'd like you to meet one of our product creators who successfully leveraged her avatar to sell her product to a staggering 40% of her list. Meet Neelam Meetcha.

 **"My income is much better now with fewer hours of work."**
Case Study from the Field: Neelam Meetcha

About eight years ago, Neelam Meetcha got very ill. So ill that she was forced to stay at home for more than 18 months. During her recovery time, Neelam worked on creative projects to pass the time with her sisters. As she worked, she tapped into a natural passion for creativity that she'd always had, but never nurtured.

After she recovered, Neelam decided to go out on her own. Although her background was in lecturing, she also decided to offer her creative talents for hire, launching a gift-wrapping business. Within three months of going live, Neelam had her first inquiry from a large nearby shopping center. She continued to grow and now works mainly for large corporate clients, including *National Geographic*.

After running this business for several years, Neelam began to realize that her business relied too much on *her*. She wasn't going to be able to increase her income unless she could leverage her time. Around that same time, Neelam also discovered she had a knack for helping other women transition from the corporate world to launching their own small businesses. She just needed a more streamlined solution to offer. Sitting down face-to-face with each client was simply something she didn't have time for.

When Neelam heard about Make, Market, Launch IT, it was exactly what she had been looking for. "It was like it was written for me. This was exactly what I needed in my life, so I purchased it without any hesitance," Neelam says.

Neelam first big breakthrough happened when she was defining her ideal clients.

She struggled with the concept initially. "I just felt like—'Why would I leave a certain group out? Why would I target just one group?' But I realized that if I target one group, it will be easier for those people to find me, so I can become a big fish in a small pond, instead of the other way around," Neelam shares.

This made the creation process significantly simpler for her. "Once I started doing the module on the avatars and the exercises in the booklet, I realized that there was a specific woman who I was aiming for. When I figured that out, I was able to create my product around that woman, which made everything easier," Neelam explains.

After putting a product together that would speak to her unique audience, Neelam launched *Business Success for Women* in July 2012.

Her commitment to this product is personal. "I'm very passionate about a family and [being] a businesswoman. I'm even more passionate about helping women to make sure that they have that quality time to spend with their family through having their own information products."

40% of her list has already purchased it. She couldn't be happier: "That's a good income for me because it's automated, I don't have to do anything." This passive income puts Neelam ever closer to her goal of working three days a week to spend time with her family, including her two teenage daughters.

To continue this initial success, she's committed to fostering the relationships she's established by finding more and more ways to serve her audience.

"It's not just about producing a DVD and sticking it on the shelf for people to buy. It's about developing the relationship. I think that's so important because these people aren't just going to be your clients or your prospects. They're going to be people who will come back to you again and again for you and your products," Neelam says.

Developing these products has had a huge impact on how Neelam runs her whole business, which offers a suite of services to women, from career and business consulting to creative coaching, including an online gift wrapping training course which includes over 35 different techniques. As part of her offerings, she used to host groups of 10-15 women in person. "I didn't enjoy that because I didn't feel like they were getting everything they wanted because it's too much of a group—and my mind is still thinking, 'I know I've got inquires coming through and I can't get through to these people, or they can't get a hold of me.'"

Now, by offering that same content online, these women have unlimited time to review Neelam's content, wherever they are in the world. With existing clients in the UK, Hong Kong, Africa and India, the potential for growth into these markets is extraordinary. The online format has also freed up Neelam's time to continue to develop her business, take care of her customers—and spend time with her family.

She only wishes she would have had access to all the information the product provides sooner. In her words, "I was really surprised that I hadn't known about any of this years and years ago because if I had, I would be a millionaire by now."

She has big plans for the future, but, even now, Neelam feels "blessed because my income is much better now with [fewer] hours of work." Her product sales have already improved her business revenue by 20% and she is confident those numbers will continue to rise.

These blessings have given rise to unexpected labors of love, like a book of poetry she'll be publishing this year, called *Poetic Challenges of a Woman Entrepreneur*. The book was inspired by all the family moments she gets to enjoy now that she has a home office, after 20 years of working away from her home.

Because, at the end of the day, for Neelam, "It's not just about going out there, reeducating yourself, making loads of money. Life is too precious to just do that." It's about finding the balance within her own life through her business—and helping other women to do the same.

In 2012, Neelam Meetcha more than doubled her holiday sales compared to 2011. She continues to expand her businesses at **BusinessSuccessforWomen.co.uk** and **GiftWrappingCourses.com.**

Step 3: Money
Create Your Irresistible Offer

The distinctions we're going to offer you in this chapter are some of the most significant we've come across. They'll help you build confidence in your business and they'll offer you final clarity on your idea. In fact, discovering them is also going to make the impending creation process that much sweeter.

Why? Because there's no better feeling than working on a product that you *know* will sell. We're not talking about gut instinct or some kind of entrepreneurial ESP.

**We're talking about cold, hard proof
that your product will succeed.**

That's what creating an irresistible offer is about.

Very few business owners begin with this process. As a result, they create products that their customers don't buy. For example, consider Crystal Pepsi, a clear cola introduced in 1992, which was the brainchild of current Yum! Brand Chairman David C. Novak. The drink was released despite research that "consumers evidently had a strong preference *against* a caffeine-free, clear cola."[14] It was later pulled from shelves after sales tumbled. It still remains a disappointment to Novak: "Once you have a great idea and you blow it, you don't get a chance to resurrect it."[15]

Microsoft tried the opposite tack, using technology to deliver customized email offers for its search engine Bing. By leveraging real-time data including location, age, gender, and online activity of the receipients, they deliver customized ads that have lifted conversion rates by as much as 70%.[16]

In other words, it all boils down to this: your success hinges on offering your prospects something they want, something they can't wait to buy. As in the case of Crystal Pepsi, success is measured in sales. In practical terms, sales are what keep the doors open. They're what compensate you for the time and expertise you've poured into your product.

But sales mean more than that...

Sales Get You Two Things

1. **Sales get your products into people's hands.**

    They're the means by which you're spreading your ideas, the manner in which you're adding value and creating change.

2. **Sales get people to pay attention.**

    Our friend, marketer Joe Polish, says: "If they don't pay, they don't pay attention."

One of the challenges you'll run into is **getting people to actually use the product they've purchased from you.** Most people believe their work is done after the sale goes through. Unfortunately, that's just not true. If your clients don't use your product, they won't receive the benefits you promised. They won't experience the value and they won't undergo a transformation.

---

14 https://gsbapps.stanford.edu/researchpapers/library/RP1977R1.pdf
15 http://www.fastcompany.com/60555/winging-it
16 http://hbr.org/2011/12/know-what-your-customers-want-before-they-do/ar/1

It also means a dead-end in your Cycle of Transformation. These people don't produce social proof. They don't tell other people about your product and they probably won't buy from you again.

But when people invest in your product, trading their hard-earned dollars for what you've got, things change.

They've got skin in the game. No one wants to waste their money, so paying customers are much more likely to follow through. Remember this principle because it's going to come up again later.

Now, it's not a guarantee. That's why it's your job to create ways for people to hold themselves accountable as they consume your product or follow your system.

But it all starts with a sale—and an investment.

Before we continue, a sobering statistic for you:

In 2004, 950,000 titles out of the 1.2 million tracked by Nielsen Bookscan sold fewer than 99 copies.[17]

That's 79%.

Do you want to be the 79%? Or do you want to be the 21%?

Because the unfortunate truth is that these numbers are not improving:

In 2011, a survey revealed that half of all self-published authors earn less than $500.[18]

That same study also showed a variation of the old 80/20 Pareto Principle in action: 10% of self-publishing authors earned about 75% of the total reported revenue.

We share these statistics with you so you'll understand the importance— and the power—of a killer offer. So you can be the 10%. You can arm yourself with the necessary tools and strategies and save yourself literally *years* of experimenting.

So what does it takes to be in that top 10%?

17 http://parapublishing.com/sites/para/resources/statistics.cfm
18 http://www.guardian.co.uk/books/2012/may/24/self-published-author-earnings

Case Study: The Power of a "Useless" Offer

Duke University professor and author Dan Ariely stumbled upon a subscription offer for the *Economist* that he was sure must be an error. Examine it yourself:

1. A web-only subscription for $59
2. A print-only subscription for $125
3. A web + print subscription for $125

Why, you might ask, would anyone choose option #2, when you can get more for the exact same amount of money by choosing option #3?

Ariely calls this a "useless" offer and even called the *Economist* to see if he could talk to the person behind the offer.

When the *Economist* wouldn't cooperate, Ariely decided to run his own experiment, to see if that "useless" offer might have some value.

He repeated the offer in an experiment and reported the results:

Scenario #1:

1. A web-only subscription for $59 – **16%**
2. A print-only subscription for $125 – 0%
3. A web + print subscription for $125 – **84%**

As expected, no one chose option #2. (Not even one crazy person.)

Ariely ran the experiment again, but eliminated option #2. The results were as follows:

Scenario #2:

1. A web-only subscription for $59 – ~~16%~~ **68%**
2. ~~A print-only subscription for $125 – 0%~~
3. A web + print subscription for $125 – ~~84%~~ **32%**

That's a pretty surprising reversal. The flip-flop demonstrates pretty clearly that a **seemingly "useless" offer very well might have a function**. As Ariely argues, the "useless" offer had a purpose: to demonstrate the value of offer #3.

In other words, when shown together, it looks like option #3 offers you web access for free. But take it away, and option #1 looks like the better value.

More importantly, let's just run the math and assume a total of 1,000 people buy from each scenario:

Scenario #1	Scenario #2
16% @ $59 = $9,440	68% @ $59 = $40,120
84% @ $125 = $105,000	32% @ $125 = $40,000
Total Revenue: $114,440	Total Revenue: $80,120

Hmmm, that's a total difference of $34,320. That's the power of a "useless" offer.[19]

To read more about Dan Ariely's work, check out his book, *Predictably Irrational*.

Your Offer Is Your Means of Survival

All too often, products are created because someone has an idea they're passionate about. Passion is an essential ingredient in the process, one that will keep you motivated to make progress. The challenge emerges when you *assume* your product will sell because you're in love with the idea.

Have you ever sat across the table from a blind date and mentally felt like he or she was planning your wedding before you'd even finished your entrées? As you would in a long-term relationship, you've got to see if your offer has wings before you get out there and make a long-term commitment of time, money and resources.

Here's why: a bad offer will doom your product.

You could have the most amazing product on the market. Your product might bring about world peace, or solve climate change.

19 http://www.economist.com/blogs/democracyinamerica/2009/05/the_independence_of_
irrelevant

But if you present it with a bad offer, no one will buy. No matter *what* you're selling.

So, here's our challenge to you.

You *think* you should be asking questions like these:

- "What format should I use to create my product?"
- "What price should I sell it for?"
- "What should I name it?"
- "How much is it going to cost to get it done?"

But the questions you *should* be asking are:

- "Have I implemented it?" (Will the money tree I am offering actually grow?)
- "Does it work?" (Will the bank take the money it produces?)
- "Do I have proof it works?" (Can I show people my bank statements?)

Unless you can share your product idea in a way that answers these questions for your prospects, people won't buy. In contrast, if you can connect with potential customers, give them certainty that your product will solve their problem, they'll open their wallets and buy.

As you answer the questions above—you'll also discover one crucial thing about your product:

***You'll* know with absolute certainty that you can sell it.**

That is power.

But before you can assemble a killer offer, you need to make some final decisions on what exactly you're selling.

The 7 Elements of Your Product and Offer

It's time to put a stake in the ground and start to map out the specifics of the product idea you're working with. Once you make some decisions in this area, we can show you how to construct a killer offer to sell it.

Let's begin:

1. **What is your product?** What exactly are you offering? A book? A teleseminar series? An online learning course? A membership site?

2. **What's the working title?** *Hint*: to save yourself a great deal of time and stress down the road, we suggest your title makes clear 1) what your product does and 2) what benefits it offers. If you look back to Sue Ferreira's case study earlier in the book, her title can make a great model for you: "Live Your Retirement Dream." For inspiration, go to Amazon and type a few keywords that describe your product and scan through the results.

3. **What's the solution you're offering?** In other words, what's the problem you're solving and how are you solving it?

4. **What's the format you're using to deliver your product?** Is it a 6-week teleseminar series over the phone? A 12-week subscription to your membership site? Will your customers receive the item all at once, or over a period of time?

5. **What's the structure?** In other words, a solution doesn't happen in a single step. This book is laid out to deliver the seven steps you need to create a profitable product. What steps will you offer your customers to ensure their success?

6. **What are your bonuses?** We've referred to the concept of delivering value early and often. One way to deliver value is to include additional items in your package to increase the likelihood of your customer's success. What else can you include in your package at no extra cost to your clients? The best bonuses are things that overcome an objection someone might have from buying your product or some kind of shortcut that will help your buyer get a desired result faster.

7. **What's your intended price point?** This is a tricky issue for even the most experienced marketer. For now, make a guess and back it up with some competitive research. We'll show you how to refine it in the next couple of pages. You'll also want to check out the most common challenges with pricing.

3 Common Pricing Mistakes

#1: Setting the Price Too Low

Everybody loves a bargain, but people are suspicious of a bargain they can't see, touch and verify.

Let's say you're standing in Macy's and there's a table full of men's dress shirts that they're trying to get rid of for bargain-basement prices. You'd pick one up, feel the fabric, test the buttons, eyeball the stitching and try it on. If everything looks good, you'd grab a bunch and walk to the counter feeling like a smart shopper.

There was a part of you that still might have been suspicious. You didn't simply trust the fine people at Macy's and not bother to check out the shirts. You examined them carefully. Even with this verification in place, you may still have felt a little tense as the clerk was ringing them up. Did they really scan at the same price as the sign promised?

Now let's say you saw the same bargain on the Internet. If it was featured on some no-name website with no credibility and no return policy, you'd probably skip it. And even if you found them on Macys.com, wouldn't a small part of you wonder, "What's wrong with these shirts that they're selling them so cheap?"

It's the same with your product.

People will always look for value, no question. But when it comes to solving an important problem in their lives, they won't always jump for a bargain-basement solution. In fact, they may be suspicious of it.

#2: Setting the Price Too High

If you present it right, a high price can increase the perceived value of a product. Although it's not always true that a $40 bottle of wine tastes better than a $20 one, we generally believe there's a correlation between price and quality.

However, there's a caveat: the price still has to reflect the value. And, in fact, we would argue that your product should always deliver immense value over and above the price paid for it. When it's the other way around, products don't sell.

A study from Cornell University recently confirmed what we've always suspected: a higher price may mean that people perceive your product more favorably, but it doesn't mean they'll buy it.[20]

Given that our equation is that sales = success, we'd call this a failure.

#3: Not Benchmarking Against Your Competition

It's always smart to know how you compare in the market. If the Internet has done anything, it's made every single one of us a comparison shopper. Whether you want to be the low-cost or the high-cost provider hinges on your branding and the package you're offering, but it's always wise to know how you compare to your competition. You can bet your customers will do their research—and they'll expect you to address any gaps within your sales process. Anything less may leave them confused and unwilling to buy from you.

When in doubt, we suggest selling at a higher price to attract the type of quality customer you'll enjoy serving. A larger margin will also free you to over-deliver value without counting every single penny. Finally, aiming a bit higher—in both price and quality—will help you stand out in your niche.

---

20 http://www.cbsnews.com/8301-505125_162-31041136/high-prices-affect-perception-of-quality-but-not-sales/

Now before you assemble your final offer, you need to do *one more thing*: you need to test it. (Note: if you play this right, you'll actually defray some, if not all, of your product creation costs.)

The Science of Product Creation

We've always admired our friend Mike Cline, founder of the firm Tech Guys Who Get Marketing, and his team because they're a rarity: technical-minded guys (and gals) who really do understand marketing and sales objectives.

When we mentioned this to him, he said something we've never forgotten: "I'm not a marketer. I'm a scientist." He tested hypotheses, he explained. If they worked, he kept doing them. If they didn't, he replaced them with something new.

In this next step for creating a killer offer, we're going to ask you to channel Mike Cline and his team. Put on your goggles and your lab coat. It's time to do some testing.

Zero Money To Get Started: The Secrets For Getting Someone Else To Pay for Your Product Development

Every world-class product goes through a testing phase. Yours should be no different.

During a beta test, ask yourself…

1. Will it sell?

2. Does it work?

3. What kind of results does it produce?

Think about how valuable it is to get these answers *before* you plunge a ton of time and resources into your product. Also, since the people you'll be putting through your beta test will be paying customers (more on that below), you'll actually be getting paid to develop your product.

Sound good? Here's how beta testing can work for you.

7 Steps to a Beta Test That Produces Actionable Results

1. **Get a Prototype in Place.** This *does* mean that you need to have the majority of your content ready, or if you're producing a piece of software, a workable version that people can use.

   It *doesn't* mean that you must have your packaging ready—or even your delivery system. For example, if you're offering an online learning system, you might deliver it as a series of webinars through a service like GoToWebinar, or as a three-day live event.

   Whatever it takes, devote some resources to getting your content in place because it's time to see if it works!

2. **Decide on a Price.** You'll want to put paying customers into your beta test, even if you're tempted to offer your beta test for free. Here's why:

   > **#1: You *never* want to devalue anything you do, especially to a group of potential customers.**

   > **#2: You need people who are committed to this program.**

   Remember Joe Polish's quote: "If they don't pay, they don't pay attention"? If they haven't invested real money, they're not going to value your product or go through the program like a real customer and give you the kind of feedback you need.

   It's *fine* to give your testers a limited-time introductory rate, such as 20-30% off the final price of your polished product. As an incentive to participate, you also may want to promise them access to the finished product at no extra cost.

   The second biggest reason you're asking people to pay is you'll use this beta test to pay for your product development, which will put you leaps and bounds ahead, cost-wise.

   What's better than getting paid to actually create your product?

3. **Enroll 10-20 People in the Test.** In addition to helping with the cost of development, you need to finish your beta test with 1) an understanding of whether your product works and 2) the proof

that it does. Enrolling between 10-20 people (or more, depending on your market) gives you more assurance that enough people will finish the program and, of that group, some will see results.

If you have trouble selling even 10, this will tell you something. You might need to rethink your idea, your delivery, your target market, your price, etc. Tweak and try again.

Our friend and #1 *New York Times* bestselling author, Jorge Cruise, uses a version of this model to write his books. He posts on Facebook, Twitter and Google+ that he's going to do a series of free seminars on how to lose belly fat. People show up, he teaches his system and eventually a group of people emerge who follow the process and lose weight.

He uses them as proof his system works in his books, brings them on media tours and tells their stories to the media to promote his book—and it works.

4. **Survey Participants Up Front.** An up-front survey is crucial. You need to know exactly where people started so you can get a baseline for improvement. This is also a great opportunity to get a peek inside the heads of your ideal clients and see how close you got with your avatar.

5. **Deliver the Product & Check-In as You Go.** This is the moment of truth: share your product with your clients and see whether the magic happens.

Develop a relationship with these clients as you work together. If you're up front and authentic with them, they're more likely to forgive any of the issues that could come up during a beta test.

You'll also want to check-in with them frequently to find out how they're doing. Ask whether they have any questions. Discover what other resources they might need. Gather as much intelligence as you can while you're in front of this group. Then, use it to refine your final product.

6. **Survey Again to Capture Feedback and Testimonials.** Here's where you'll (hopefully) get some candid feedback on your clients' experience to help you improve your final product. Don't forget to ask for testimonials. An "after" survey is a great chance to easily collect the social proof that will become vital in creating your offer. This is a perfect opportunity to offer existing customers a discount if they upgrade to the next product in your escalation path.

7. **Make a Plan for Improvement.** The biggest mistake people make with survey data is *not using it*. Don't let this happen to you. Take a few days to get some perspective, then read through your customers' responses. You don't have to incorporate every piece of feedback, but do pay attention to the common themes. Then, plan your changes accordingly. One very powerful strategy is to be transparent with your data. Make a video and present the results you're comfortable sharing publicly so your prospects and customers feel as though they're part of the creation process themselves.

And voilà, your beta test is complete!

This process should help you find answers to the three vital questions about your product:

1. Will it sell?

2. Does it work?

3. What kind of results does it produce?

With these answers in hand, you're ready to construct your killer offer.

The Mafia Offer: Making a Killer Offer Your Prospects Can't Refuse

As you go through this process of building an offer that makes your target market open up their wallets and buy, there are two elements you need to pay attention to that are happening simultaneously:

1. The structure of the offer and how you present it.

2. The psychological formulas behind what you're presenting—the psychology of influence.

The Art of Influence

We find the psychology of influence fascinating. If you share our enthusiasm, we suggest you check out these books as a start to further studies:

- *Influence: The Psychology of Persuasion,* Robert B. Cialdini, Ph.D.

- *Pitch Anything,* Oren Klaff

- *Predictably Irrational, the Forces That Shape Our Decisions,* Dan Ariely

- *Thinking: Fast and Slow,* Daniel Kahneman

When we're creating offers for our own products, we start with these:

The Four Ps of Creating a Killer Offer

1. **What is their problem?** You have to both understand and articulate the problem to your audience with the clarity of the Millenium Star Diamond. In other words: flawlessly.

2. **What is your promise for how you will solve their problem—permanently?** You also need to articulate *exactly* how your product will get them out of their situation, now and into the foreseeable future.

3. **What kind of irrefutable proof do you have that your product produces results?** Here's where your beta test will pay off. What real-life examples, stories or case studies you can share as proof your product works?

4. **What is your step-by-step process to solve the problem?** Although people do want a quick solution to their problems, they don't want quick fixes. They want—and need—a system, a step-by-step plan for going from Point A to Point B.

And here's where the psychology comes in: people want to be their own solution.

Let us clarify. Despite the persistence of the myth of the knight in shining armor, most people are not looking for you to swoop in and solve all of their problems.

They want you to show them how to solve their own problems.

They want the motivation and the strategies to be the heroes of their own lives. They want to be empowered to make a change.

Remember, you're entering these peoples' lives to help them make a lasting change, whether you're offering a training program or a widget. Unless you're planning on moving in next door, you can't always be around. Giving someone the tools they need to become the hero of their own lives is the greatest gift you can give someone. It may seem counterintuitive, but when you give people this gift, they'll actually love you *more* than they would if you were acting as their white knight.

If you can incorporate this concept within your pitch—and give your ideal clients the power to be their own solutions—you'll have an offer that practically sells itself.

Before we close this chapter, we want to introduce you to Rob and Michael Doxey. These two creators saw firsthand how powerful the right offer can be, especially when beta tested. Rob and Michael's story also offers you a glimpse into exactly how these Make, Market, Launch IT strategies play out in the real world.

 ## "We felt it would be easier to scale."
Case Study from the Field: Rob and Michael Doxey

A few years ago, brothers Rob and Michael Doxey started Vampas Marketing to create online marketing and video solutions. Although this proved a lucrative business for them, they wanted to significantly increase their revenue potential without expanding their operations.

Inspired by Make, Market, Launch IT's step-by-step system to simplify the creation process, they decided to pursue a business around information products.

"We felt it would be easier to scale once we figured out a system and were able to get some momentum," Rob says.

In short, Rob and Michael were ready to stop trading time for money.

"Once you've created [a product], and you've created your system, you can't sell out of it, " Rob continues. "Especially if it's digital, you can sell as many as you can sell. Whereas, with [Vampas Marketing], that's not really true. You have to add employees, or you have to have the structure in order to grow."

Rob and Michael have already created three different products, both on their own and in tandem with other creators. Make, Market, Launch IT has "definitely been influential. The thing I love about Pam and Mike is that they have a ton of experience. But, they don't just have experience, they have actually had success—they've been able to turn profit on their products. You're learning from people who not only teach it, but they do it every day."

Rob and Michael's first product was *Mastering Mealtime*, designed to help busy, multi-tasking moms succeed in the kitchen. From the beginning, they focused in on how to add value to a specific audience, leveraging Michael's background as a chef.

"[The product idea] wasn't really about my skillset, it was more about a problem I saw, and the problem was that moms were very stressed out every day about what to make for dinner," Michael explains.

After Mastering Mealtime, Rob and Michael went on to create a second product with a partner they met at a Make, Market, Launch It event. The result, *Pranayama Running*, has already exceeded the success of *Mastering Mealtime*. They credit Make, Market, Launch IT's strategies with making the difference.

"The most impressive thing to me…is just how amazing [Pam and Mike] were at being able to put together an offer. Understanding exactly who your customer is was one of the biggest things I took from it," Rob says.

Make, Market, Launch IT also helped to streamline Rob and Michael's process. "Just the structure of how [Pam and Mike] do everything is so critical. If you have formulas and you have a framework, the time it takes to create additional products is drastically reduced. For example, *Mastering Mealtime* vs. *Pranayama Running*—it's night and day in terms of how long it took us," Rob explains.

In addition, Rob and Michael learned how much beta testing could improve the quality of their offer. *Mastering Mealtime* didn't go through a beta test, and their sales suffered. In contrast, before launching *Pranayama Running*, Rob and Michael are doing a significant amount of beta testing, and their results are promising.

After getting "phenomenal results from the focus group," Rob and Michael have also taken the idea to Icon Health & Fitness, creators of the Nordic Track, to explore possibilities for expansion. They secured the meeting based on principles they learned at the Make, Market, Launch IT live event in May 2012.

Their advice for others ready to create or launch a product? Don't create your whole product until you've gotten real feedback from real customers. In fact, they are currently working to tweak their offer for *Mastering Mealtime* to make it more compelling, based on the lessons they learned with *Pranayama*.

As Rob explains: "We didn't do a beta test before launching *Mastering Mealtime*. Later, we did a focus group, and they didn't pay. For *Pranayama*, they paid. And that in itself is a huge difference."

Rob and Michael are currently still in the process of tweaking the *Pranayama Running* offer to accommodate the needs pinpointed during their beta testing. "It's so important for us to get it right in terms of understanding who the real target market is," Rob explains.

Make, Market, Launch IT also reminded them how important it is to speak to their audience in its own language. This is particularly critical, they believe, in explaining the offer in a way that is meaningful to that audience.

"That's a big, big takeaway—talking in a concrete way and not in an abstract way, " Michael says. "Instead of saying, 'You're going to be happy when you use *Pranayama Running*,' you've got to say, 'You're going to have more energy so you can run that extra mile with no problem,'" he continues.

Rob and Michael are in the process of creating a third product with the working title, *Zero Risk Trading*, a combination of an information product with software. They're excited to finish the development phase. "There's nothing in the marketplace in the stock market like it," Rob says. Their role will mainly be in the marketing and sales of the product itself. "Some of the content creators frankly don't know anything about marketing," Rob says. That's where he and Michael—and their Make, Market, Launch IT experience—come in.

As they work to launch (and re-launch) each of their products, Rob and Michael are continually drawn to the freedom the information product business model has given them, as well as the ability to make a difference in the lives of others.

"I think the big thing is, it gives you freedom," Rob says.

In Michael's words, "Five, ten years down the line—I see myself doing what I love, and that's creating products that help people, and doing it in a compelling way. I would like to make my work impact people's lives and make a good living while I'm doing it."

Mastering Mealtime is currently available at **MasteringMealtime.com**. *Pranayama Running* (**PYRunning.com**) and *Zero Risk Trading* will launch in 2013.

Step 4: Leverage
Get the Best Resources That Save You Money & Time

Being an entrepreneur can be a solo endeavor: you and your vision, going it alone.

That's why the two of us feel so lucky to have found each other as friends and business partners.

We keep each other focused. We keep each other on track with our goals. We lean on each other when the going gets hard—and we celebrate together when we hit a home run.

As your ideas take shape and your business grows, you need to reach out to "trusted advisors" and people who will give you honest feedback. You can't do it *all* on your own, even though there are times that it might feel easier to do everything yourself.

Entrepreneurs are often, by nature, lone wolves. When you do everything 100% by yourself, you know it will get done the way you want it. You also have to take take the time to make it so.

This chapter is about sharing the responsibility by getting leverage. As Archimedes, the Greek mathematician who invented the lever, said: "Give me a place to stand and with a lever, I will move the whole world."

It's also about discovering the fastest path—and least number of resources needed—to achieve your core business outcomes.

In addition to establishing a support system to help you recognize, tackle and process the challenges of entrepreneurship, you'll also need to assemble the resources to make your ideas a reality.

This includes the money, the people and the systems that will fuel your enterprise.

Especially when you're first starting out, we're big fans of bootstrapping. By using limited resources in a *smart* way, you can get by with minimal overhead. That's why we talk about strategies like beta testing which allow you to get paid to create your product.

This is your ideal scenario. You won't have a big debt hanging over your head or a stack of bills waiting on your desk. When the revenue starts flowing, you'll hit the black much more quickly. That money is *yours*, not the bank's, not an investor's.

Bootstrapping definitely has its benefits, although you won't need to bootstrap forever—unless you want to. Ultimately, this idea, this product and this business are all about *you* and what you want. Use your revenue to set up a business that supports the lifestyle of your dreams. That's why the ultimate leverage is a business that runs without you. And if your ideal involves getting even greater leverage and spending more time out of the office, we're big fans of that, too.

But when you're starting out, keep your expenses low.

In the long run, being fiscally conservative will always serve you.

It will keep the pressure low. It will keep running your own business *fun*. And if you set it up right, it will mean more profits for you to enjoy.

For a moment, it's time to turn your focus inward again to understand the business that you'll build around this idea.

It's time to understand exactly what you want from your Make, Market, Launch IT business—and how to get there.

Your Monthly Burn: A Story from Mike...

Several years ago, my company started doing online product launches. Our largest generated $9.1 million in revenue in a single week, including over $1 million in 43 minutes and $2 million in sales in 1 hour and 14 minutes.

That's a great story. Here's the downside.

I started taking my eyes off the business. Every problem that came to me, I did my best to offload it onto an employee or a contractor to solve it. It soon became apparent that I wasn't managing our money. People started to take advantage of this and pretty soon low-level employees were getting paid twice what the industry rate was for that job. We went from 20 employees to 60—plus contractors. Our overhead grew to over $500,000 per month.

Our monthly continuity revenue from our software services was about half that amount , so it meant we had to "clear" several million dollars a year just to survive.

And then the bad news came: one of our merchant providers—the middleman between your credit processor and the bank—decided to hold back $1.2 million of our cash indefinitely. More bad news: my CFO announced to me one day that we would run out of cash in less than two months.

Suddenly, I was on a never-ending cycle of having to do product launches in order to survive. A few months later, I was hit with a massive tax bill that exceeded the amount of money I drew from the company for the past two years.

It took over a year to decrease expenses, downsize, get rid of one-sided contracts and plug what seemed like an eternal list of unreasonable expenses.

The week my team and I got the company finances under control, I was diagnosed with cancer.

The good news? Thanks to having a second business with my partner Pam, a great customer database, continuity income, the ability to launch and release new products and a competent team that ran the business while I went through surgery, chemotherapy, radiation treatment and all kinds of complementary and alternative therapies, we remained stable and profitable.

But I learned an incredibly important lesson that I had heard but not heeded for years: "It's not what you make, it's what you keep."

It was my fault. I took my eyes off the ball. Filled with hubris and a sense that I could always make money no matter what happened, I was suddenly given the "gift" of a life-threatening disease that gave me perspective.

The morals of the story:

- Business is a combination of relationships, permission and trust.
- Your list is your life-support and the gift that keeps on giving. Build a business you love, serving customers you love to serve.
- Keep your expenses low.
- Live below your means.
- Don't give someone else control of your checkbook.
- Build a business, not products and focus on creating continuity/subscription income.
- You're getting older much faster than you realize.
- Get it done. Those who hesitate go out of business.
- Don't quit until you're ready.
- Build a business someone will want to buy, even if you never sell it.
- Learn from your mistakes.

The good news is I've made a huge health turnaround and my business had a record year despite only being able to work 20% of my normal pace and being mostly out of the office for nearly six months. That's the power of setting your business up right. It's never too late. Start now.

That's Where Leverage Comes In

True leverage is about maximizing your resources. It's about making your business efficient and effective through discipline and focus. It's about about creating results while simultaneously making your life *easier*.

Getting leverage is mandatory before you move into full-on product creation mode. It allows you to do several things:

1. **Create the best-quality products** for the least amount of money in the least amount of time. Money loves speed.

2. **Set yourself up for future success** so that each new product adds geometric growth to your business.

3. **Avoid the major business challenges** that can eat up your profits, negatively impact customer experience or damage your reputation in your industry.

Getting this leverage for yourself and reaping the rewards happens in three phases:

1. **Defining your core business objectives.** *What do you want? How will you get there?*

2. **Creating a project plan.** *How exactly will you achieve these objectives? What steps will you take?*

3. **Securing the right resources.** *Who and what will help you get there?*

Getting leverage for yourself is one of those cases when a little planning up front will ensure that you're on the right path to your ultimate vision.

The opposite—lack of planning—can spell disaster: unanticipated expenses that eat away your profits because you're doing things last minute.

If you don't plan for what you need—and *when* you need it—you won't be able to get the best resources at the best price. Lack of planning might mean that your preferred contractors are already booked. If you can convince them to squeeze you in, it could cost you a bundle in rush fees instead of regular rates. Or it might result in your second- or third-choice contractor executing your job, producing a less-than-impeccable result. You might even end up doing the work yourself, which isn't always the right use of your time.

Plus, when you're executing on the fly, you end up working reactively. Timelines go out the window as you microfocus on what needs to get done in the moment. Stay strategic. That's where leverage exists. There's no way to gain maximum leverage and be tactical at the same time.

All these scenarios mean added stress for you. You end up frustrated because things aren't going the way you wanted. Your team may feel frustrated because you don't have the time and focus to give them the direction they need to execute to your standards.

And, ultimately, the biggest loser in this scenario may be your customer. If you end up sending a product to market that's not impeccable, they won't get the value or the results they'd hoped for. This, in turn, will start to affect your brand and your reputation in the marketplace. You'll also pay for it in increased refunds, support challenges and your long-term sales.

But you're here now. You've already taken a significant step toward preventing these challenges. Let's take the next step together and plan for your success. Let's get leverage.

Giving yourself full leverage requires you to take a critical look at your to-do list and decide which actions support your vision. Which directly contribute to that vision and your core objectives? Those are the things you need to continue to do.

If there's anything on your to-do list that doesn't support your vision, it's time to simplify. Stop spending your time, energy and resources on these items. Let them slide off your plate and don't look back. Your customer will never know the difference and after a bit of time, neither will you.

Now that you've reached an understanding of what you want for yourself—and for your business—let's discuss how to get there. It starts with a good plan. There's a formula for this too.

Pam's Project Planning Essentials

Just as we're all about simplifying your to-do list, we're also about simplifying the project planning process. The idea is to create a strategy for completion that clearly delineates the timeline and the owner of each element to keep your product on track.

After executing projects of every size, shape, urgency and importance, I've discovered...

More Time in the Planning
= Less Time in the Execution

The alternatives cause some serious challenges. Lack of planning almost ensures that your project will be late—and likely over budget. However, the opposite—in which almost as much work is put into the plan as the project itself—will cost you time and energy that you could have put into the product itself. Staying strategic pays dividends.

Planning for success starts by identifying four key elements in advance:

1. **The ultimate outcome of the project.** It's paramount that everyone involved 1) clearly understands and 2) commits to being on board with the result you're working to achieve.

2. **The overall owner of the project.** Who is the accountable and responsible person for making sure the project is completed on time and on budget? Because this chapter is all about leverage, keep in mind that this could be somebody other than you. You could hire a project manager to oversee this, especially if project management is something you don't particularly enjoy or excel at.

3. **Key milestones, their deadlines and their owners.** What are the individual steps that must be completed along the way in order to achieve the ultimate outcome of the project? What date do they need to be complete? And who, specifically, will own each one?

Take a lesson from my experience: each milestone should be owned by a single person. Shared responsibility simply doesn't work. Psychologists have a word for what happens when more than one person shares the same task: diffusion of responsibility. You've probably heard about the studies showing that people are almost three times as likely to take action in emergency situations when they're alone as opposed to when they're in a group.[21] It's the same with your project. Two people sharing a milestone will naturally assume that the other person is watching out for it. Keep your project from becoming an emergency situation and delegate each milestone to a single person.

4. **The resources you'll need to complete the project.** This includes the people, money and systems you'll rely on. We'll discuss strategies for securing these resources shortly. The key, as I stated at the start of the chapter, is to secure these resources *in advance*, to ensure efficient use of your time and your money.

Designing Your Project to Work for *You*

One of the great joys of being an entrepreneur lies in designing your own working lifestyle to support the way you work. You're in charge now. It's your prerogative to set up the systems that support the positive emotions of your life: joy, excitement and passion. As you do this, we offer you a couple of tips to support you as you support yourself.

1. **Make sure you leave yourself some breathing room.** By planning a little wiggle room at the end of your project, you'll create an environment that's ready to handle a couple of snafus. When they happen, and they do, cushion you've created will help keep you calm and resourceful.

---

21 Cited in: http://en.wikipedia.org/wiki/Diffusion_of_responsibility

2. **Use a system to track progress that works for *you*.** The market is full of project management systems. We've used everything from Excel spreadsheets to fancy, full-scale software. The key is choosing a system that works like you do. If you're an analog person at heart, a giant sheet of paper with key milestones and their dates might work best for you. Technology does offer a number of advantages, such as being able to share that giant piece of paper with your team and automatic alerts to keep everyone honest. Just make sure that it's not creating more work to track your project than it is to actually execute it.

3. **Offer clear rewards and celebrate when the project is complete.** One of the biggest dangers in the entrepreneur lifestyle is burnout. This is especially true if you're always racing from huge project to huge project. This is true for your team as well, particularly if you're using the same contractors over and over again. Wrap up every project with the appropriate acknowledgments, thank yous and rewards.

Now that we've laid the groundwork for completing your product on time and on budget, let's discuss how to get you the leverage to start taking action.

 When Projects Go Wrong...

...and they inevitably do in some form, the key is not to panic. You can't make good decisions when you're in a state of panic. Take that emotion and focus it toward your ultimate outcome. There's always another way. If you take a step back in a resourceful state to consider the bigger picture, another path will appear. Perspective is key—in the grand scheme of things, you're going to be fine and nobody will remember your mistakes anyway.

Ultimately, anticipation is your best weapon. For every major component of your project, ask yourself and your team: "What could go wrong?" Create a plan for dealing with these potential challenges in advance. If you can anticipate potential challenges to the point where you can prevent them from happening, even better.

If you get stuck along the way, consider bringing another resource to the table. A brainstorming session with a colleague can shed new light on an issue. A project manager can clear your plate of the responsibilities that are keeping you from hitting your deadline.

Finally, remember *why* you're doing all of this. Connect yourself to your vision and recognize the future you have in front of you. Then, come back to the present and take the next step you need to get on track.

The Three Levers
Money • People • Systems

Money is a resource. Like all of your other resources, you have to manage it to get the most out of it. As an entrepreneur, you have the unique opportunity to have a direct hand in the decisions that affect how much money you put in your pocket at the end of the day. It's all up to you.

It all starts with a detailed financial plan that will show you the resources you have on hand, the amount that's coming in, the amount that's going out and how much you'll have left over at the end of the day.

Even if your intention is to ultimately delegate your finances to an accountant or someone else within your company, you need to keep a continual pulse on your business. Why? Because no one will care about the financial future of your business as passionately as you. That passion drives the small corrections that keep your business in the black.

The Game of Business

At a minimum, you must understand these four numbers at any given time:

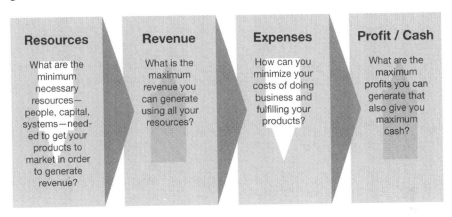

Resources	Revenue	Expenses	Profit / Cash
What are the minimum necessary resources—people, capital, systems—needed to get your products to market in order to generate revenue?	What is the maximum revenue you can generate using all your resources?	How can you minimize your costs of doing business and fulfilling your products?	What are the maximum profits you can generate that also give you maximum cash?

You must understand where you are in these four categories in order to effectively manage your business.

You can delegate the nitty-gritty details to someone else. However, you should never lose sight of these four numbers. We've seen too many friends get burned by leaving them entirely to someone else.

And, don't forget, accounting has its joys, too! You'll want to be there to log your first dollar of profit into your books—and all the others afterward. It's one of the pieces you've been working so hard for, a tangible one that carries a lot of meaning. Celebrate it.

Assembling Your Financial Plan

You'll start your planning process by identifying your risks and developing projections for the upcoming year. These two elements will allow you to make more intelligent decisions for your business in the future.

Look at the first three categories in the chart above: resources, revenue and expenses. Given what you know about your target market and the offer you're planning on making them, project your numbers in each category.

When we make our projections, we embrace this philosophy: hope for the best and assume the worst. When you're developing an overall vision for your business, aim for the stars. Anything less doesn't serve you. But when you're calculating the numbers behind it, project low. Worst case, you'll meet your numbers. Best case, you'll have extra money to put away. This will keep you away from the deadly cash crunch.

Given your projections, what's your profitability looking like? Go back and adjust the three categories as necessary to produce your desired profitability.

As you work through this financial planning process—particularly on the resources and expenses side— ask yourself two questions:

1. Does your customer really care? Is this mission critical to getting the outcome they desire?

2. Is this the best use of resources (time and money) right now?

If the answer is "no" to either question, consider postponing that expense or resource for another time.

 Accountant's Corner: Tracking Expenses

There are three types of costs that are important to track:

1. Product development costs

2. Marketing costs

3. Delivery costs—the cost per unit to get your product in the hands of the customer, e.g., the cost of goods on a physical product.

Make sure you track each of these separately so you can accurately determine your metrics and make effective decisions about your business moving forward.

Why? Because your **development costs**—the one-time costs to make the product—need to be tracked separately from recurring costs. This way, you'll understand exactly how quickly you've made back your initial development investment.

Your **marketing costs**, when measured separately against your sales numbers, will give you a good idea of the effectiveness and quantitative return on investment you're getting from your marketing activities.

Your **cost of goods**—any expenses relating to the production, storage or fulfillment of your product—will tell you what your ongoing margin is.

Lump all these costs together and it will be tough for you to see where you can afford to cut (and increase your profits).

The Three Levers:
Money • **People** • Systems

Next let's take **advantage of the second lever: people.** In these next pages, we'll ask you to think about who can step in to free up your time, so you can focus on the things that only you can do.

Getting people leverage is also about freeing yourself up to focus on the things you want to do. What brings you joy? What do you look forward to tackling? When you can outsource efficiently and effectively, you can do more of the things you love and fewer of the things you don't.

Ultimately, that's the end game of this entire book. Getting you leverage for your *life:* creating products to bring in revenue to free up your time so you can enjoy the things you love. It's an exciting thought, one that we hope keeps you inspired throughout the process.

As you leverage people to help you, you'll be joining good company. In a recent survey by the website Elance, 42% of employers said they anticipate hiring more freelancers in 2013 than the previous year.[22] Their reasons are as varied as the types of functions you can outsource[23]:

1. Gain access to resources or expertise unavailable internally: 49%
2. Reduce or control costs: 44%
3. Free up internal resources: 31%
4. Improve business or customer focus: 28%
5. Accelerate company reorganization: 22%
6. Accelerate a project: 15%
7. Reduce time to market: 95%

Easiest Functions to Outsource:

- Accounting and bookkeeping
- Advertising campaign design and management
- Audio editing
- Copywriting for marketing, advertising or promotions
- Customer service
- Graphic design
- IT support
- Marketing strategy and execution
- Personal/virtual assistant
- Research
- Search engine optimization
- Software design
- Video editing
- Web development
- Writing, editing or proofreading for content

22 http://management.fortune.cnn.com/2012/11/27/freelance-jobs/
23 http://www.statisticbrain.com/outsourcing-statistics-by-country/

Discovering Your People Needs

When you're making decisions for what you want to outsource, sometimes it's easiest to work backward. We've found it helpful to reverse-engineer the situation so you can understand 1) what needs to get done and 2) who should be doing each function, while maximizing your resources.

Ask yourself these key questions:

1. What are the **core functions that must be done each day** to manage the day-to-day operations of my business?

2. What are the **core projects will help me achieve the five major outcomes** for my business (e.g., a specific product launch, etc.)?

3. Out of everything, **where is my personal time best spent**? What do I enjoy doing the most that adds the most value to the growth of my business?

4. Therefore, what other **functions ideally would be handled by other people**? Number these in priority.

5. What is your **maximum monthly budget** to spend on people resources supporting the day-to-day functions of your business?

6. What is your **maximum monthly budget** to spend on people resources supporting your key current projects or product development efforts?

   (*Hint*: The answers to these last two questions will come from the budget you've created.)

Once you know the answers to these questions, you can generate a list of the people who you will approach for help and set a maximum monthly budget for paying each person.

The Three Levers:
Money • People • **Systems**

Every business has overhead. The key is deciding what you need to invest in and what "nice to haves" you can pass on, especially when you're starting out. (Remember the study we cited in Chapter 1?)

One of the best ways to make this concept real is to calculate what we call your *Monthly Burn*.

Your Monthly Burn is the minimum amount of money it takes to keep your doors open.

This includes everything: your contractors, production costs, website subscriptions, anything on which you pay out money.

This is a key number to know. The larger your Monthly Burn, the more products you need to sell to be profitable.

As we mentioned earlier, you don't have to bootstrap forever if you don't want to. Creating your own business is about designing your own personal lifestyle. If you dream of an office where you can be creative uninterrupted, rent one. If having an assistant significantly improves the amount you can get done, hire one.

Just keep in mind that anything you spend on the front end will ultimately reduce the profits coming out of your business. Discipline will keep your Monthly Burn low—and reduce the pressure on you to sell at least X number of units a month.

We suggest evaluating your overhead Monthly Burn to "trim the fat" and remove excess expenses where they don't matter.

This is especially true where office space is concerned.

Although we agree on many things, both of us approach this aspect of our business differently. Mike has a full office and a studio where he does all of his filming. Pam mostly works out of her home office, as does her husband.

Where you work—and how you work best—is up to you. Shared office spaces are popping up all over the country, providing people a retreat from their homes without the steep rent or long-term lease of your own commercial space.

The truth is: your office does say something about how you run your business. If you avoid both extremes of extravagance and scarcity—in how you run your business and furnish your office—you'll settle into a balance that serves you, your team and your clients.

To wrap up these concepts of leverage, we offer you the story of Bruce Jones, one of our Make, Market, Launch IT creators who was inspired to become "a one-man international company." See how Bruce is getting leverage in his own business while expanding his suite of products to free up his time to spend more with his family.

 **"I can be a one-person international company."**
Case Study from the Field: Bruce Jones

When Bruce Jones's younger daughter started college, he decided it was time for a change. After almost 30 years of working as a graphic designer, he was ready to move from the "laying-out-newsletter" clients. Bruce was ready to shift the focus of his business more strongly toward developing online products and free up his time.

Bruce was no stranger to selling online products. He had long supported his freelance career by selling editable clip art maps to everyone from graphic designers to sales teams creating PowerPoint presentations to religious groups planning their missions. He had also branched out into books.

"I have 19 books now that I've done," he says. "They range from music books for guitar, mandolin, ukulele and banjo to geography books." He also has a series of coloring books. All of these, he created through Amazon CreateSpace.

However, after jumping into Make, Market, Launch IT, Bruce had a couple of realizations.

First, he knew he wanted to expand and do more consulting. After seeing the strength of his books, Bruce had a stream of authors ask for his help in publishing their own works. Bruce also looked at a course he'd taken with a video journalist back in 2008 and saw the incredible potential to help it go global. And, finally, although Bruce had always developed products to support his freelancing, he was ready to grow.

"I've been selling $49 products," he realized. **"I want to sell a $149 product.** You can create books, and software and products and sell them online, and be basically a one-person international company. The power is really amazing."

Bruce took action. He pitched his idea for an online product to Bill Gentile, a veteran reporter with a deep bench of experience in foreign correspondence that included covering the Sandinista Wars in Nicaragua for *Newsweek*. After taking Gentile's Backpack Journalism course in 2008, Bruce had stayed in touch and was helping Bill with his social media.

Make, Market, Launch IT helped him realize the full potential of Bill's content—and their partnership.

It wasn't always an easy sell for a traditional journalist like Bill. "Most of these people have never done anything like this," Bruce says. "They're kind of suspicious. They don't know how it works. [To them,] YouTube is just cat videos and skateboarders."

Bruce used Make, Market, Launch IT to show Bill how they could partner up and put it all together. It was the *avatar* exercise, the Make, Market, Launch IT concept around building a visual image of your ideal client, that sealed the deal for their venture. Once they knew who their ideal client was, it was easy to create a product with that type of person in mind.

From there on in, Bill was on board. Bruce modeled MML strategies to help Bill completely revamp his site, creating an "Essential Tips and Tools" opt-in to attract more subscribers. He started seeing results immediately. Enrollments for his intimate workshops had been dwindling to 3-4 people. The new website started filling his workshops to capacity.

To keep moving forward, Bruce knew they couldn't do it alone. **They would need leverage.** "It takes a team," he notes. "I've tried to do it by myself with my book publishing product. I'm just by myself, and I discovered it's almost impossible. A team is really powerful."

"You don't need a big team," he continues. "You need a producer, which is my role. [Bill Gentile] is the talent. We have a web guy and we have a couple other people floating around. But you can be guerrilla at it. Don't go crazy spending a zillion dollars."

Together, they're filming the main content for the course in front of a live audience in late 2012.

That wasn't the original plan, he notes. They tried to film by themselves initially, but discovered that Bill needed an audience to stay on track. They reworked their strategy. "We have real students paying real money. Pam mentioned that. That's something I learned [from her]: Have some real people in front of you."

Bill Gentile's project is just one piece of Bruce's overall plan for his business. "Think global, act local," is his current product development philosophy. "There are a lot of potential buyers out there. You want to put stuff out in many, many different ways."

For him, that means continuing to develop bigger, higher-price-point products—with bonuses. "It was a huge insight when I saw what [Pam] did: 'Here's the welcome letter, here's the product, here's an expected bonus, here's an *unexpected* bonus,'" he says. "I was like, 'Oh, what do I have that I can throw into my box?' I went running around my office going: 'What can I put in my box?'"

It also means continuing to expand his consulting business, as well as a publishing product to complement it. Many of his clients are aspiring authors who want to get their books published, while others want help with video creation and marketing.

For the confidence and strategies to take on this work, Bruce credits Make, Market, Launch IT, which he calls "very, very helpful in terms of being a consultant. It helped me organized my thoughts. **The avatar workshop, the product funnel, the questions about the product, the personal psychology, those worksheets… were very, very helpful."**

Bruce also sees great potential to expand into other fields formerly dominated by more traditional marketing—or no marketing at all.

"I play guitar and mandolin and I go to this Summer Acoustic Music Week Camp here in Boston every year," he says. "There's so many budding folk acoustic musicians out there who are brilliant musicians but struggle with the marketing. And you can have a global reach as a musician immediately just making YouTube videos."

He offers a final note: **"Anybody can do that in whatever field you're in. You can design products that are distributed for free or that you can make money from. That's a pretty cool thing."**

Bruce Jones and Bill Gentile's online course, *Video Journalism Workshop*, is expected to launch in early 2013. Live courses are currently available at **VideoJournalismWorkshops.com.**

Step 5: Create
Structure, Produce & Package Your Content

It's time. Are you ready to translate your knowledge, know-how, expertise and experience into a product that will transform people's lives? Are you eager to show your customers your own unique blend of strategies and tools that will solve their deepest problems, add value and create visible change? Are you excited to put your stake in the ground and begin the core process that will turn you into a highly sought-after expert and creator?

We are—and we hope you are, too, because it's time to start creating. And the good news is that everything you've done up until now will make this process easier and more effective.

If there's a "trick" to product creation, it lies in *balance*.

On one side, you've got the wild, exciting, unpredictable, exhilarating and elusive creative process.

On the other side, you have the very practical need to 1) make your content useful to your audience and 2) complete your product in a timely manner.

It's the perfect intersection of your right brain and your left brain.

In order to create a truly great product—an innovative solution that produces real results—you'll need to blend both forces with dexterity—and patience. You'll dive into the creative process full-on and discover things about yourself that you never even knew. You'll also come to see your expertise in an exciting, new light. You'll see it as though it's the first time you're experiencing it and there's nothing as exciting as rediscovering that passion.

You'll get in a groove. Your fingers will fly over the keys, or you'll get a burst of energy that your pen simply can't keep up with.

As we said, it's unpredictable and thrilling.

That's why you need to stabilize the creative portion of this journey with structure and planning: to keep you going consistently, to deliver on the small steps that lead to momentum and, most importantly, *to ensure that your brilliant ideas get translated into a product that delivers for your clients.*

In this chapter, we'll show you how to create content that sets you apart in your field, content that delivers on its promises to your clients and creates lasting change.

This is the heart of the process. It's also our favorite—because this is where passion, science and art meet.

In this step—your ultimate outcome is this:

To provide your customers content that is relevant and useful to them—information that stands out from everything else that's available because you are creating a personal connection and helping them fulfill a need or solve a problem quickly, effectively and permanently.

Everything you've done up until now has led to this moment. Let's get started.

What Are People Really Paying You For?

Most people believe they're being paid for what they know.

In a way, that's partially true. Your expertise is an ingredient in the package you're offering, but that perspective doesn't reflect the whole story.

Information is everywhere. It's on the ads we're bombarded with as we cruise the Internet or walk down the street. It's on our phones. It's on flatscreens in the back of taxicabs.

Every *minute* on the Internet:

- WordPress users publish 347 new blog posts
- 571 new websites are created
- YouTube users upload 48 hours of new video
- Apple delivers 47,000 app downloads
- Google receives 2,000,000 search requests[24]

Every *minute*.

It should come as no surprise in a recent survey we did of the members of our email list, 62.5% cited "eliminating overwhelm" as an urgent need.

So, when it comes to attracting clients to your product, what's going to help them reduce their overwhelm?

What will set you apart and mark you as someone your customers will look to?

Knowledge helps. Credibility helps. Branding helps. But these alone aren't enough to set you apart and get you a piece of the $272,070 spent every minute on the Internet.[25]

Here are the three things that will:

1. Leveraging the Power of Perspective
2. Owning Your Humanity
3. Empowering Your Clients to Produce Results

---

24 http://www.visualnews.com/2012/06/19/how-much-data-created-every-minute/
25 http://www.visualnews.com/2012/06/19/how-much-data-created-every-minute/

Master these three and you won't have any trouble dominating your niche. You'll stand clear of your competition. Your voice will ring loud and true as one of abundance and authenticity. You won't have to fight for customers because they'll be fighting to work with you.

We'll show you exactly how it works.

Leveraging the Power of Perspective

How you see the world—and your customers—is something that's uniquely yours.

It's your *perspective*, and it's a powerful tool to set yourself apart.

Your perspective is a product of your unique knowledge and experience. No one can duplicate it and no one can take it from you. Own it, and you'll be offering your clients something 100% unique, something your competition can't copy, no matter how hard they try.

Have you ever felt like all the good ideas are taken? Or that it's challenging to create something totally new?

We know what you mean. We talked earlier about how much information is available in the world today—data that is now measured in a unit called "exabytes" (whereby each one is equivalent a billion gigabytes) because there is so much of it. If you just look at the data we're bombarded with as individuals, each of us encounters the equivalent of 174 newspapers worth of data per day. Think back to our example of stacks of data on DVDs going from the earth to the moon and you've got a sense of how much data is being generated. And, yes, you can learn how to do most things by Googling them.

That's where the power of perspective comes in.

To every topic, new and old, you bring a unique mix of knowledge and experience to the table. This mix forms the lens through which you see the world. Your lens is unlike anyone else's and offers you the chance to bring a fresh perspective to an oft-discussed topic.

For example, let's take the topic of how we, as humans, make decisions. It's already a crowded market—remember, this is a good thing from a marketing perspective—but, depending on your experience, you could approach it from a number of angles:

- You could come at it from the side of *economics*: What are the basic economic principles acting upon our decisions?

- You could come at it with the perspective of *neuroscience*: How is the brain processing this data?

- You could come at it *sociologically*: What are the human forces influencing our choices?

- You could explore it as a *parent*: How are your toddlers learning to decide for themselves?

- You could examine the *influence of technology* in expanding our choices: How do Amazon and Google change our buying patterns?

And we're simply speaking in general terms. If the one-and-only you decides to tackle decision-making behavior as a parent, your result would be significantly different from your neighbor's.

The door is wide open to you, just for being *you*.

Whatever your hard-earned expertise, wear it as a badge of pride. That's what will draw people to you and help you create a product that's uniquely yours.

Owning Your Humanity

Our humanity is our greatest gift, especially in the product creation process.

Think about it from someone else's point of view. Put yourself in the shoes of your avatar who's in the throes of her problem. Imagine yourself appearing with empathy and compassion, offering a way to connect and—through all these things—a solution.

When you lead with your humanity, it gives people hope. It inspires them to be something greater. They feel connected. It also makes them listen to what you have to say.

Consider an example: Who would you rather take a challenging yoga class from? An ethereal, frosty instructor who has no problem bending herself into a pretzel and can't seem to understand why you can't do the same? Or a warm, friendly teacher who tells you a story about falling out of a headstand in front of a class of inner-city teenagers?

Humanity—and our inherent flaws—are what help us form connections. They're what make us real.

Author Brené Brown has taken this idea one step further. Years of sociological research led her to discover that vulnerability is a key ingredient in forming human connections. What makes us human, in other words, brings us together. If you can embrace your vulnerability, she believes, it can be the "birthplace of joy, creativity, belonging and love."[26]

When you accept your imperfection with grace and authenticity, you'll become relatable to your customers. You become a real person who they can form a connection with.

You'll also attract more people to you because, ultimately, we're all looking for acceptance. Acceptance for who we are, warts, flaws and all. By being an example of imperfect humanity, you provide your clients the permission to relax and be who they are. You'll become someone meaningful, someone they can believe in.

Own your humanity—and encourage your customers to do the same. They'll love you for it. It will make you feel good, too.

One of the ways that you can bring a human element to your content is by making room for storytelling.

Telling stories is one of those basic human activities that allow us to exchange information while deepening our connection with ourselves and with other people.

Your customers also want to learn lessons for themselves, rather than being told why things are. Stories allow the listener to filter their experience through his or her distinct lens, allowing them to have their own unique experience with what you're teaching.

Empowering Your Clients to Produce Results

Creating lasting change starts with a simple step: getting your customers to open the package they ordered.

---

26 http://www.ted.com/talks/brene_brown_on_vulnerability.html

Then, once they tear open the box, log into your membership site or attend a workshop or event, their success depends on them using what they've purchased by taking action continuously until the desired results are achieved.

In other words, your ability to create results rests on making your product simple—and compelling—to use.

For example, let's say you create a three DVD multimedia program that you ship to your customer's house. What will make her open up the shipping box with excitement? What kind of box will entice her to break the plastic overwrap and look inside the package itself? What will get her to pop in the first DVD, right there and then? What will convince her to follow through on the content you present? Then, what will bring her back to DVD #2?

You need to consider how your customers will consume your product at every single step. Anticipate their roadblocks and eliminate them. Recognize points where they may get discouraged and offer them a support system. When motivation may start to wane, note these spots and reinforce follow-through.

When you've considered your product from all of these angles, while standing in your customers' shoes, you can create a product that will get lovingly consumed—and will deliver results.

Although it might seem like the creation process ends with a sale, that's when the experience *begins* for your customers. Your long-term success hinges on your ability to see your customers through the process, long after the money has cleared your bank account.

Content That's Structured to Deliver

Structure is the key to driving results.

A good structure makes it clear exactly what your customers are supposed to do, when they should take these actions and in what order. It takes your customers by the hand and leads them through your content, step by step, making it simple—and enjoyable—to complete your entire program.

Structure also combats overwhelm, which will be your customers' biggest challenge to completion. But before you even start to create the core structure of your content, you need to identify two things:

1. **The outcome of the content you're delivering.** What are you trying to deliver to your customers? What effect are you hoping to have?

2. **How to deliver it for maximum impact.** How can you present this information in the most effective way to achieve that outcome?

These two concepts form the essence of content creation. Let them be your guide as we dive into the core structure of your product.

Create Your Foundational Structure:

1. What are the steps that you'll take your customers through to get them from where they are now to where they want to be?

2. Are these in the right order? Could a different sequence produce a better result?

3. Put yourself in the shoes of someone just starting out. Could someone who's completely new to this topic follow this sequence with success? Add in any steps that might be missing.

4. Look back over your list above. Are there any steps you could eliminate or combine?

Your Content Template

Once you decide on your overall steps, it's go time! You've done all the planning you need, so get ready to share the meat of your expertise with your audience. To get you started, we want to share with you a few distinctions on what's worked, both for ourselves and for others, when creating a product that leaves its mark.

We believe there's a basic formula to delivering content with impact. After creating countless presentations, video scripts, blog posts—pretty much anything you can imagine—these seven steps emerged as the most efficient and most effective way to get a point across. In fact, you'll recognize these techniques in use throughout this book.

As you gain experience, you may develop your own tricks and variations. No matter your level of experience, we think you'll find this a solid base for conveying information, no matter the format or audience.

The 7 Step Formula for Delivering Content with Impact

1. **Share What It Is.** Set people's expectations for what they're going to learn from you. As we mentioned earlier, this becomes an implicit promise that will establish your credibility when you deliver. If possible, show the result first, just like some filmmakers open the movie with the last scene first. It creates intrigue and keeps the viewer's attention.

2. **Explain Why It's Important.** To grab your audience's attention, you need to offer them the "what's in it for me?" Explain how listening is going to change their lives—in specific terms—and you'll have every ear and eyeball in the room.

3. **Break It Down.** As you did with the overall steps of your program, deliver your content in manageable pieces. Make it easy to digest. When people get confused, they tune out. Clear and simple content will help you keep your audience's rapt attention.

4. **Offer an Example.** Illustrate your distinctions with real-world examples that your audience can relate to. Showing your ideas in action will reinforce your credibility. If you can do a live demo, even better.

5. **Have Them Do It.** When you can engage more than one of the five modalities of learning, you can connect with your audience on a deeper level. Also, if it's possible to create immediate results through action, you'll earn incredible trust and create a lasting impression.

6. **Acknowledge Their Progress.** You can only build on success. By simultaneously 1) teaching your clients and 2) building their self-esteem, you'll achieve lasting results.

7. **Review It.** Remind them of the promise you made at the start of your presentation and emphasize its fulfillment. Then, wrap up your presentation.

Now that you've got your structure aligned for success, let's look at the best way to deliver it to your clients.

 ## The Five Learning Modalities

Everyone has their preferred mode of learning. By engaging multiple modalities as you teach, you'll open up your content to be appreciated by a wider audience. Also, when you can engage a single person in more than one modality, you'll deepen the impression your content has on them. This is why video, which combines the auditory with the visual, is such an effective delivery vehicle.

What can you do to engage these modalities within your content?

1. Auditory (hear)
2. Kinesthetic (do)
3. Olfactory (smell)
4. Tactile (touch)
5. Visual (see)

Next time you prepare to teach a piece of content, brainstorm some ideas. Experiment with the possibility of asking your audience to do something while watching (kinesthetic & visual), or ask them to repeat phrases back to you (kinesthetic & auditory).

Be creative and have fun with it! Depending on your product, you may not use all five, although imagine the power—and impact—of a culinary presentation that smells delicious.

Produce Your Content: Digital vs. Physical

At the end of the day, giving form to your ideas boils down to **delivering content that people can consume in the format that makes the most sense for your market.** Although there are numerous options for delivery, the biggest question on most people's minds today is "digital or physical?"

To clarify, we use the term "digital" to refer to an online-only version of a product, like a membership site with videos, as opposed to its physical form, which would involve DVDs and printed handouts.

Online products have many advantages when you're starting out, particularly in ease of distribution. It's also easier and quicker to create and distribute a product online (no cost of goods), and it gives you the opportunity to change or improve things more easily.

However if you're planning to sell your product in a live setting, having something physical to hand to a customer may be more effective. You'll also want to consider creating both, as we did for Make, Market, Launch IT. Almost 40% of our customers chose to upgrade and receive both online access to our membership site as well as a physical pack that included all the DVDs, printed handouts and more.

In our experience, having a physical product allows you to charge more, creates happier customers who believe you're delivering more for the money and reduces the number of refunds.

Not every business is the same—and if you're just starting out, you may consider selling a digital-only product to reduce your risk and overhead.

Ultimately, this is one of those decisions that's entirely yours—and it will depend heavily on the market you're serving.

Once you decide how you're going to deliver your product, there are a few other things you'll want to consider:

1. **What format will help my clients absorb and apply the information? Audio? Video? Written?**

Your answer will depend heavily on your avatar. Some will love video. Others will clamor for handouts. This is where knowing your ideal customer becomes vital.

You'll also want to consider providing content across modalities to support individual learning styles. For example, within the Make, Market, Launch IT online program, we offer videos, PDF summaries and audio downloads. We suggest that you choose a primary presentation style (video, audio or written) and then use at least one element from each of the other two styles to reinforce it. For example, if yours is a video-based program, consider providing audio as an option as well as handouts to review your main points.

2. What tools can I offer to reinforce my content?

Would templates help people apply your information and follow through? Could you include summary cards they can carry with them on the go?

Portability is a huge consideration in our increasingly mobile society. People want to access content on their devices from anywhere in the world. What can you create to support a busy multi-tasker who's on the move?

3. How will I create interaction with my customers?

Whether it's within your core format (i.e., a Q&A session during a teleseminar series) or packaged alongside your content (i.e., a customer forum for questions within a membership site) make sure you offer your customers a way to interact. Interaction creates "stickiness," meaning that it encourages people to keep using the product you're offering.

Just make sure you encourage interactivity in a way that supports your ultimate business and lifestyle goals. For example, if you don't have the time to monitor and support a forum, either hire some help or choose another method for interaction. In the last chapter, we'll show you how to recruit your customers into a Power Tribe who can help you with this.

Content Check: Seven Easy Pieces

Regardless of the format you choose, we've identified seven basic components you need to include to set a solid foundation for a product that communicates your ideas in a way that's easily understood and eagerly consumed by your audience.

To create a product with long-range impact—one that can guide people toward long-lasting change—you'll need a full package that reinforces success at every step, in multiple formats and modalities. We've come to rely on this seven-piece checklist that forms the basis for every product we do, whether the price is $97 or $4,997.

After you've decided on your format, round out your package using the checklist below. In addition to ensuring that your product is cherished by your customers, it will also help you round out your offer and entice more potential buyers.

1. **Welcome, Introduction & "How To":** *Where to start, what to do and how to do it. Have you given your clients a clear welcome that shows them where to begin?*

2. **Core Content Chunks, Broken Up into Steps:** *The heart of the material you're delivering. Are your steps as clear and simple as they can be?*

3. **Reinforcement Tools:** *Additional resources in different modalities to reinforce your content. How can you help your clients absorb your material easily?*

4. **Action Tools**: *Exercises and templates to create follow-through. How can you encourage your clients to take action toward change?*

5. **Bonuses:** *Announced & unannounced items to help create success. What can you offer to create surprise and delight?*

6. **Escalation / Upsells:** *Next steps for clients looking to deepen their relationship down your Client Path. Where will your clients go from here? Just be sure to wait until you've massively delivered on your promise before offering more products or services.*

7. **"Stick" Content & Plan:** *The way you'll ensure that your clients keep using your product and see results. What will keep them coming back, step after step? What will prevent refunds and returns?*

Ask yourself: what missing pieces do you need to add to your product?

Once you've decided on these seven pieces, we suggest making one final survey based on one of the core concepts of Make, Market, Launch IT: *value.* Look back at the offer you created in Chapter 3 and ask yourself: does the final incarnation of my content deliver on my promises?

And, more importantly, does your product deliver value *over and above* the price you've decided on?

If your package seems wanting, either go back and augment your content or reconsider your price point. Or, better yet, rework your product so that it delivers beyond the investment you're asking people to make.

With this final check in place, it's time to take the final step: deciding on the packaging that you and your customers will love.

Packaging Your Product

You can't separate your content or your product from its delivery. In other words, the packaging has as much to do with the customer experience as anything else you do. Put serious thought into the contents of your "box of stuff" as well as to the overall look and design of the packaging, whether you deliver your product online or offline.

As you consider the limitless array of options for packaging your product, there are three areas for you to consider:

1. Brand execution
2. Perceived and actual value
3. Production and fulfillment costs

We'll start with your first consideration: branding.

Brand Execution

Branding is the overall image you are portraying with the design, quality and execution of your product. Each of these says something about who you are, so it's important to know what message each component shares.

1. **Create your packaging with an eye to detail.** Even the way you present your name matters. Will you be "Dr. Jane Berman?" Or, as one of our creators has done, will you identify yourself in a less formal way—"Grandpa Jack"—to relate on a more personal level?

    The same goes for your product name, as well as the look and feel of the product itself. What does each piece project? Try to put yourself in the shoes of a stranger and look at your packaging design. What messages does it convey? What promise does it hold? And, more importantly, do those outward messages match the inner contents of what you're offering?

2. **You'll also want to examine your package from your ideal customer (or avatar)'s point of view.** Will it appeal to "Melissa?" Will she be so thrilled to open it that she'll rip off the plastic and dive right in? Will she get the results she desires?

    At the end of the day, your package should say: "Open me! Use me! I'm the missing piece you've been looking for!" Your branding is a huge part of this.

    Your presentation also has a huge impact on what happens after your customers open the package, including whether they believe they got what they paid for. That's why it's so important to understand your product's perceived value.

Perceived Value vs. Actual Value

Your packaging has a huge impact on whether or not your customers believe your product is worth its price.

We package our products with the goal of inspiring a "wow" factor. Even across varying price points, we always aim to create a high perceived value in relation to the investment. Of course, you'll need to back up your perceived value with *actual value* by delivering on the promises you've made, but if you've followed our recommendations for creating your content, this will be a snap.

When running your business, you'll also need to consider perceived value alongside your budget goals to ensure that margins are large enough to create a profit. Especially if this is your first product, we recommend being conservative with your packaging costs.

One way we've struck this balance is by choosing fewer components of higher quality. The old "quality over quantity" rule generally creates happier customers and protects your margins.

However, make sure not to package too many things together. Keep a few items separate, to make sure people realize all that they're getting. While it's wonderful how much you can fit on a single DVD, it can really affect the perceived value of your package. For example, if someone pays $997 for a product, but it's packaged on one compressed CD-ROM— even though it's 400 pages of material and 12 videos—it won't feel like much to the customer.

And, yes, the box matters. So does the look and feel of your online product. Make sure that your product inspires an emotional reaction in your customers from the first moment they see it. (Just make sure it doesn't kill your budget at the same time.) Preferably, this is a message of warm welcome. When you deliver, you're a guest in someone's home. Package your product to invite them warmly into your world.

Once you feel confident that you've created the right emotional and rational reaction to the value of your package, there's one last set of factors that you need to consider: your production and fulfillment costs.

Production and Fulfillment Costs

The way you manage your final production and fulfillment costs— and, frankly, the expenses that pop up throughout—can make or break your business. As you deliver amazing, life-altering content to your customer base, it's important that you make a return on your hard work. This is it: the chance for you to get paid for your hard-earned and well-deserved expertise.

Managing these costs is the key to making this equation work for you. It's what will provide not just the revenue, but the profits that fund your lifestyle. Make smart decisions at this stage in the process and your rewards will be not just great, but tangible.

1. **Watch out for hidden costs.** It may seem like a few dollars here and a few dollars there, but little costs can really add up. For example, if you've already sent your product to a production house and you notice a mistake on the proofs, it's going to cost you money to change it. Or if you want to change some of the look and feel of your membership site—even if it feels like tweaks to you—those costs can creep up quickly. Every time you contemplate adding to the cost of your package, re-run your numbers again. Are you still making money at the price point you've anticipated?

   You're ultimately aiming for an 8:1 or a 10:1 return on your investment. If you're not hitting these numbers, take a hard look at your costs. Is there any way to trim expenses without making a significant sacrifice in quality? Ask yourself the two questions we posed earlier: Does the customer really care? Will he notice? What's critical to delivering your content? If you really want to profit in this business, you need to be willing to cut and manipulate components as necessary.

2. **Ask questions.** What you don't know is your responsibility to find out. You can't ask enough questions. You don't need to know everything, but you do need to know enough to be able to manage the whole process. You'll also want to make sure you get a sample or a prototype before releasing anything to the public. Ask your production company up front about this before you make a commitment.

3. **Be prepared to negotiate with your vendors.** When you bid a project out to two or more production houses, you may be surprised in the variation in prices. Ask questions of the lower-cost options and get a prototype if you can to make sure the level of quality is up to your standards. As for the higher-cost providers, tell them about your lower bids and ask about the difference in price. They may be willing to come down or be able to explain the difference in what they're providing.

4. **The cost of your packaging may feel like a minor detail in this process, but it's not.** Your margins will ultimately determine how many products you need to sell to create the business—and the lifestyle—that you desire. Good margins will make it significantly easier, as long as the value is there for the customer. Low margins are every creator's worst nightmare; your return simply won't feel as worth it to you.

However, if you follow the advice we've offered in this chapter, and you're able to control your costs wisely, you'll be well on your way to profiting from your expertise—and a giant leap closer to creating the sustainable business of your dreams.

To inspire you as you put your package together, we'd like to share the story of Make, Market, Launch IT creator Jeffrey Goodman. Make, Market, Launch IT helped him structure his course for results, creating both happy customers and speaking opportunities around the world.

"Make, Market, Launch IT [gave] me the tools to organize 30-plus hours of content into a very manageable product."
Case Study from the Field: Jeffrey Goodman

Jeffrey Goodman was comfortable with his success as a fashion-advertising photographer, making six figures and working only a few days a month. However, in 2003, his photography career took a very unexpected turn.

"In April, I took a class in energy healing just for fun," Jeffrey explains, "and by July, every aspect of my photography business was gone: my assistant of eight years moved to New York, my stylist of six years decided to take a two-year sabbatical, my photo lab I had been using for ten years closed and I lost all my clients."

"It was very surreal for me because at the exact same time this was all happening to my photography business, I had this very fast growing waiting list of clients wanting to see me as an energy healer." Jeffrey notes. "People have commented on how it was an obvious sign from the universe. Perhaps it was."

After seeing Jeffrey's initial success, other healthcare practitioners, including doctors, chiropractors, acupuncturists and alternative energy healers started coming to Jeffrey for advice. They wanted help creating the kind of success Jeffrey had. He was more than willing, **"I love helping people succeed and showing them how to discover their true potential."** He also had plenty of experience, after providing business consulting and development services to photographers and artists.

By leveraging this expertise, Jeffrey began to teach healthcare professionals how to turn their craft into a thriving business. "Just like in the world of creative artists and photographers, there are so many amazing health practitioners who are very talented at their craft—and yet they do not know how to integrate their skills into running the business side of their practice," Jeffrey explains. "They were never taught the specifics necessary on how to start or grow a successful business."

Jeffrey began teaching professionals how to interact with their business as a "living energy"—in its literal sense. "It became very clear to me that just like a person can be stressed or can get sick, so can a business. [This] allows us to diagnose where their business is healthy and where it needs care and attention."

As demand grew, Jeffrey sat down and developed a three-day live training course and workshop he calls *CareerHearted*.

The big question that came up over and over again was: **"Is it online?"**

When he encountered Make, Market, Launch IT, Jeffrey knew it would provide him with everything he needed to take *CareerHearted* to the next level of success: 1) the framework to repackage his product and 2) the system to promote and sell it successfully.

By applying the steps he learned though the Make, Market, Launch IT program, Jeffrey was first able to reorganize his content into its current incarnation: a seven-step program based around the seven chakra energy system of the human body. **"Make, Market, Launch IT [gave] me the tools to organize 30-plus hours of content into a very manageable product."**

"Organizing the *CareerHearted* course in this way allows me to show people which aspects of business relate to which chakra. For example: in the Root Chakra, I talk about the business foundation and topics like money. I walk people through how to set prices for their services as well as how to address any of their fears and issues with money," Jeffrey explained.

The reaction so far has been incredibly positive. **"People over and over tell me how much *CareerHearted* has changed their businesses. Surprisingly, it has also dramatically changed their lives,"** Jeffrey reflected. "I have had several couples tell me privately that this course radically enhanced their marriage as well."

After repackaging *CareerHearted* and relaunching it to his existing audience, Jeffrey went from speaking locally in Phoenix, Arizona, to now speaking and teaching globally, almost overnight. "The other day I had people from over 11 countries watching my first live online introduction to the *CareerHearted* course," Jeffrey explains.

Having a product has also presented him with exciting new opportunities.

"I just got back from teaching *CareerHearted* in Canada, and I leave tomorrow to teach in Australia and New Zealand. In the next few months, I'll head to South Africa, the United Kingdom, Ireland and Netherlands. I was also invited to share *CareerHearted* in Germany, Hong Kong and Singapore," he notes.

The best part? **Jeffrey's program is making a huge impact and helping more than just healthcare practitioners transform their respective businesses.** *CareerHearted* has also had significant impact on lawyers, insurance agents, business strategists, authors, personal chefs, accountants, university professors, web developers, restaurant owners, personal trainers, dentists—and even the senior minister of a church, all of whom were looking to evolve the way they do business.

Jeffrey is now negotiating with several international organizations about white-labeling the *CareerHearted* course as a required course for their members. "Make, Market, Launch IT helped me polish something I had, and gave me the confidence that I was ready to launch it on the big stage: the online stage. It gave me the checklists I needed to succeed, and helped me avoid costly mistakes I would have otherwise learned the hard way," says Jeffrey.

As he looks down the line, Jeffrey is excited to finish the online version of *CareerHearted*. He credits Make, Market, Launch IT with showing him that "I have everything I need to take this to the next level of success, with the proper structures in place in the back end to support its growth."

Make, Market, Launch IT gave Jeffrey one more significant piece of support that he didn't realize he needed: "I already had a product called *CareerHearted*. I already had the common sense of business success. **Make, Market, Launch IT gave me the checklist I needed and the confidence to say: 'Okay, *CareerHearted* and I are now ready to launch ourselves to the next level!'"**

Jeffrey Goodman's online products start launching in early 2013. Find out more about *CareerHearted* at CareerHearted.com.

"The greatest good you can do for another
is not just to share your riches but to reveal
to him his own."

—Benjamin Disraeli

Step 6: Launch
Promote Your Product & Build Your List

You're standing at the cusp of greatness.

You've got a value-adding, life-changing product finished and in your hands. Congratulate yourself for achieving this huge milestone.

Now it's time to get your product out there in a major way. As you embrace this process, you'll step ahead of your peers. You'll move into the realm of the top 10% who significantly outearn their competitors. You'll never have to worry about being the creator of a garage full of products, the author of a dusty trunkload of books or the owner of the world's greatest online learning membership site with a user base of three people.

Your potential is limitless when you launch your product the right way.

The word "launch" can carry a number of different connotations, so we want to be specific.

> **When we say "launch," we mean** *getting your product out there in a big way,*

…whatever that means for your particular business.

For many companies, product launches play a significant role—and with good reason: launches are gaining significant traction. A study in 2008 revealed that 69% of surveyed Americans couldn't remember a single new product launch. In 2011, this number dropped to 43%.[27] In other words, people are paying attention to product launches now more than ever.

Your expertise, your product and your ideal client avatar are unique to you, so your launch will be different from everyone else's. More than anything, we don't want you to feel the pressure to compete, especially when it comes to launches.

Competition is good, when you view it through the right lens. Competition means there's a market for your idea. It means that there's a big enough group of people out there who are willing to spend their money on the problem you want to solve.

Competition is only "bad" when you let it intimidate you. Especially when you're in the early phases of a new business—or creating your first product—it doesn't make sense for you to compare yourself to someone who's been in the business for 10+ years. If you keep at it, you'll get to that level, especially with the right strategies supporting you. But the business equivalent of "keeping up with the Joneses" won't serve you.

That doesn't mean that you shouldn't model what other people have done. Examining successful launches—especially when they feature similar products for your avatar—is a great way to shortcut your way to success. After all, why stumble through the dark, when you can already see what's working and use similar strategies in your business?

And before we get too far, we also want to be clear what we mean when we say "model." We don't mean "steal." We don't mean "copy." And we don't mean "plagiarize."

What we do mean is: do your research. Take a look at your competition. What are they doing? What seems to be working for them? What kind of posts on Facebook seem to get a great response? Which of their videos are getting 1,000+ comments online?

---

27 http://mmnpl.wordpress.com/2010-results/

Then ask yourself, "*Why?*" What elements of content strategy, marketing, sales and psychology are resonating with their audience? How can you adopt similar strategies?

Once you know what other people are doing, carve your own path, inject your personality, your vision—and prepare to put yourself out there in a big way.

Raising Your Profile

It's time to give your product the attention it deserves. Especially if this is your first time doing a big promotion, it's heady stuff. It's where all of your hard work pays off. All those years of experience and ideas culminate here: in large-scale, multi-channel promotion.

Have you ever had someone come up to you and say, "You changed my life?" It's an incredible opportunity—and a rare gift. By launching your product into the marketplace, you have the chance to add value and change lives on a large scale.

But, launches are not for the weak of heart. Putting yourself out there in a major way can be stressful. In addition to the sheer number of resources and the amount of effort you'll contribute, launching means exposure.

It can be a challenge psychologically, especially if you're a natural introvert. Your business may just be you and your computer, or you and a small team of people. You may not have even told a single soul that you're building a business, or maybe you only told your family and a few close friends.

Now it's time to share your story with the *world*.

You might feel a tiny bit of fear at this step, which is okay. Fear can give you energy. Just don't let it keep you from taking action. At this point, assume you have created a fantastic product that's going to add incredible valuable to your client base—and form the solid foundation of your Make, Market, Launch IT business. Here's the good news: once you launch, most of your work will be done. All that's left is implementing the final steps that create ongoing income for you with much less effort.

To set you up for that future, we'll show you how to launch your product by maximizing your message across as many promotion channels as possible to take advantage of the resulting momentum. That's the essence of an effective launch.

But, as we'll show you, launches aren't meant to be a long-term business strategy. Your initial introduction to the market will require significant effort up front. However, when you can maximize this effort, it will produce momentum, allowing you and your team to continue to produce results with fewer resources.

If you were to look at the revenue graph of a company who relies exclusively on product launches, it would look like the Rocky Mountains. All huge peaks and valleys. If you rely exclusively on launches versus ongoing marketing strategies, that will also be the psychological profile of your business: ups and downs. It's a frenetic way to do business, one that will come to feel like a pressure cooker, especially if one of the valleys underperforms.

Our ideal for you is to create a consistent business: one that more than pays the bills, one that provides a consistent stream of revenue, one that supports the lifestyle you've always wanted to live—and one that doesn't keep you up and night, wondering where your next dollar is coming from.

That's why, even as you maximize your initial product launch, you'll want to be thinking about two things:

1. Setting up an "evergreen" system to extend the lifecycle of your product.

2. Creating a long-term marketing strategy to keep new clients coming into your business.

Because we want you to get out there in a major way, let's start by discussing how to create an effective launch and maximize your opportunities.

Maximizing the Allure of "NEW!"

Everybody loves something new: a "new and improved" formula, a new pair of shoes, a hot new restaurant that's booked for the next three weeks straight. The smell of a new car.

In fact, neuroscientists have discovered that the thrill of the "new" is hard-wired into our brain.

A study done at the Wellcome Trust Centre for Neuroimaging at University College London showed subjects a mix of cards with symbols on them, some of which became familiar to participants over the course of the study. When the subjects chose a "new" and unfamiliar symbol, it "lit up the brain's ventral striatum, an evolutionarily primitive part of the brain and an area associated with rewarding behavior." Dr. Bianca Wittmann, the chief researcher, speculated that this choice also released dopamine in the brain.[28]

In case you're not a neuroscientist, dopamine is our reward neurotransmitter. When you got an A in fourth-grade math, your dopamine levels increased. When you lost that stubborn five pounds you've been battling for weeks, your dopamine levels increased. Some of the most addictive drugs out there, like cocaine and methamphetamine, act on dopamine release in the brain.[29]

In other words, we're neurologically programmed to feel a sense of reward when we choose something "new."

That's powerful stuff. And that's why we suggest introducing your new product with a launch—to allow you to take advantage of this piece of neuropsychology.

That being said, a couple of caveats regarding your initial product launch:

1. **Nothing less than a full-out effort will work.** In the oft-quoted words of Yoda, our favorite movie mystic, "Do or do not. There is no try."

---

28 http://www.neurosciencemarketing.com/blog/articles/the-power-of-new.htm
29 http://en.wikipedia.org/wiki/Dopamine

If you decide to go with a launch (and we applaud you!), put all your focus and energy into it. Don't do it halfway. A launch is your chance to raise the bar, exponentially increase your exposure and move your business forward geometrically. Great rewards require great commitment. Trust us, if you go out there half-ready, you'll never forgive yourself. Circle your wagons, hunker down and get ready for the fireworks. In the end, it will all be worth it.

2. **Be wary of expectations.** Mike has always said that expectations are the enemy of happiness. Yes, you will see results from your launch, but they won't always be equal to the ones that you see touted by other people.

   Here's a little secret: nothing is ever as good—or bad—as it's first reported. Make realistic projections to challenge yourself based on where you are now, not where you see other people. When you finish, take a long look at where you end up. You'll find happiness in measuring your individual progress. You'll also want to focus on results beyond revenue, including brand recognition and building your list, all of which contribute to your bottom line in the long run.

   And remember, there's always another chance to redeem yourself or improve if things don't go "just so." Tomorrow is a new day.

Now that you understand a little about the psychology of launching your product, let's dive into the specifics of the process, starting with what exactly a launch will do for your business.

Depending on what you're launching and how you're launching it, your individual goals will vary. However, there are a few things that almost everyone can—and should—hope to get out of a major product launch:

1. **Cash Infusion.** A successful launch can generate revenue more rapidly as you collect orders and generate new publicity. This will infuse your business with a shot of revenue, which may help you recoup any R&D costs or upfront investments in its production. And trust us—there are few things as exciting as watching orders pour into your shopping cart.

2. **New Partnerships.** Your product launch is an excellent time to establish new partnerships, develop friendships and foster reciprocity. By setting up mutually beneficial promotions, you'll establish ongoing relationships with affiliates who you can rely on for years to come—and who will come to rely on you, as well.

3. **A Bigger List.** As you create your launch plan, you'll want to establish methods for capturing prospects' contact data. One of the most common ways to do this is by creating an opt-in that trades a piece of content for someone's email address. That way, you can continue to market your product using email, both during your launch and long after your initial launch is done.

4. **Exposure.** As we mentioned earlier in the chapter, a product launch will put you out there in a big way. It will begin to establish you as "someone to watch" within your niche. Sooner or later, this means that people will start coming to you with opportunities, which is always a good thing. You never know when an inquiry is coming from a celebrity or—someone who knows thousands of potential customers for you.

5. **Momentum.** As your launch plan comes together, all the actions you're taking will create a kind of synergy. This buzz that you've created in the marketplace will give you momentum to 1) form even more partnerships and 2) turn even more prospects into customers. Momentum is something you can't buy. Its power for sweeping opportunities your way is unmistakable and exciting. Once you've reached it, momentum is almost impossible to stop or slow down!

Ask yourself: what are you hoping to get out of your launch?

Before the heady buzz of these benefits takes you over, there are a couple of things that you need to plan for in order to remain sane in the midst of the maelstrom.

Finding Your Calm Within the Chaos

As we've told countless partners, contractors, colleagues and friends:

"I can handle anything, as long as I can prepare for it."

When you can take these five simple actions to lay the right groundwork for your launch, you'll be ready for just about anything.

1. **Remember: Your initial product launch is a means to an end.** It's not the end goal unto itself. If—and when—things get crazy, we find it helpful to take a step back. We remind ourselves that this launch phase is just temporary. It's not our entire business model (assuming you follow our recommendations in this chapter). It's merely one way to achieve the goals we just explored. Keeping this mindset will help you stay sane in case chaos breaks loose.

2. **Expect returns.** The power of a product launch lies in its use of the psychology of influence. While this can mean a lot of sales in a short period of time, it can also mean higher than normal returns, assuming you're offering a money-back guarantee. Often times, this happens because people will buy in the heat of the moment, even if your product isn't right for them. Of course you want to minimize these as much as possible. There are things you can do to impact returns, the most important of which is making sure you over-deliver on your promises. Expecting returns now will help you plan for them, psychologically and financially.

3. **Accept help from partners while making plans to give back.** If you're able to recruit joint venture partners or affiliates to help promote your product, we encourage you to take advantage of the exposure. But even as you're accepting their participation, remember that it's a two-way street. Make plans early to give back to the people who've helped you. It's obviously the right thing to do, and it will support your reputation in the marketplace.

4. **Get your merchant processing in order.** Product launches can make banks and credit card processors nervous. They haven't necessarily caught up with the speed of commerce and don't quite know how to feel about a sudden change in your revenue. If you

haven't communicated with them in advance, they sometimes respond by freezing your money, which puts you in a difficult position, especially if you owe commissions to your affiliates. In our experience, your best bet is to ask for a referral from a colleague who's already done a launch—and to anticipate some snafus, so you don't tear your hair out when they happen.

5. **Know that like any big push, it will require some effort and energy up front.** Anything short of this, and you know you're not getting out there in a big enough way. Put everything you can into your launch, knowing that it will be over in a short period of time. When you look back on the process, you'll be glad you contributed what you did. Remember, you only get one chance to have a first impression in the marketplace with your product or service.

Your initial product launch, regardless of the format, can create massive results in a compressed period of time. By proceeding with eyes open to the possibilities and the potential pitfalls that await, you'll have a much better chance of managing the emotion and excitement with grace.

We often think of a big launch as "trench warfare," It's intense, it's tactical and lots of unexpected things happen in a short period of time that are impossible to predict. The good news is the intensity of a launch fades—and it makes you stronger.

 ## The Psychology of Launches

Product launches leverage some of the most powerful forces of influence to create an atmosphere that pulses with the message, "Buy NOW!" Because these tools are so powerful, we urge you to be transparent and authentic as you use them. Besides being unethical, anything else will damage your reputation and brand.

Here are two of the principles that are usually at work:

1. **Scarcity** – *The perception of limited quantities or number of people who can participate.*

   Scarcity leverages the fear of missing out. By building in a limit to the number of products you have available, you'll encourage people to buy now…or else risk being excluded from the promotion. One authentic way to do this is to sell only the physical products you have on hand—and vow to print no more, even if you get additional orders. If you're promoting a live class, you might enforce an enrollment limit. It takes discipline to execute with integrity, but scarcity can be an incredibly powerful influencer. Scarcity can also be a great tool to keep your commitments manageable. You never want to sell more of a product than you can reasonably fulfill. Fulfillment issues hurt Best Buy's reputation during Christmas 2011 and the company is still trying to recover.[30]

2. **Urgency** – *The perception of limited time.*

   Your initial product launch can't—and shouldn't—last forever. Setting an end to your initial product launch will not only guarantee your sanity, but it will also give people a reason to buy now, before your promotion ends. To make urgency work for you, you'll need to set a time limit on the offer you're making. For example, your product may be $24.95 until midnight tomorrow, at which time it will go up to $39.95—or it may not be available at all, an offer that combines both urgency and scarcity.

   Again, the key here is discipline. It may pain you psychologically to tell a potential customer that your product is no longer available for $24.95, but think

---

30 http://enterpriseresilienceblog.typepad.com/enterprise_resilience_man/2012/01/order-fulfillment-potential-source-of-embarrassment.html

about the message you'll be sending if you give in: that you're not a person of your word. All the trust and credibility you've worked so hard to build will crumble.

Scarcity and urgency are merely two tools that you can employ to influence another person to take action. If the psychology of influence interests you, take a look back at the resources we offered in Chapter 3 to expand your palette of techniques.

The Ingredients of a Successful Launch

Jim Rohn once said: "Success leaves clues."

We agree, which is why we've compiled our ingredients from watching launches of every size, in countless formats, with their varying degrees of success and failures. We believe modeling is a great way to shortcut yourself to faster success, and it's vital when the stakes are as high as they are in a launch.

In these next few pages, we'll share what's worked for us, our colleagues and our friends, to help you secure that same success for yourself.

It starts with a great product.

You want to go out there in a major way with a product that's absolutely amazing. It's like the old parable of a house built on sand. Launch from a foundation of solid rock—an impeccable product—and you'll set yourself ahead from the start.

That doesn't mean you need to strive for absolute, 100% perfection.

We said it earlier and we'll say it again: Perfection is the enemy of progress. At some point, it's time to stop tinkering and get into production. In other words, stop messing around and make something already. Your customers are waiting for you!

However, as we discussed in Chapter 3, even an impeccable product needs something extra.

You need to pair your product with a killer offer that will compel people to open up their wallets and buy.

Your offer will make or break your launch. But here's the good news: You can tweak it as you go. We've seen many a launch saved by a couple of significant modifications to the overall package during the launch period. It might sound like driving a car while trying to change the tires. It is— but it works.

Once you have a great product packaged with a killer offer, you need to put the right systems in place to support its delivery.

This includes a clear method for purchasing that 1) collects payment efficiently and 2) delivers you the information you need to get your product in your clients' hands. It also includes 3) the customer support systems to help them when challenges emerge.

Establish these systems early. Test them often and compulsively. Otherwise, you risk turning away a crowd at the gate. That's one of the most painful feelings you'll ever have in the product creation process.

Once you're prepared for a flood of clients, it's time to attract as many eyeballs as possible.

In other words, you need access to a significant number of prospective clients.

Marketing is nothing more than a math problem. We'll dive more deeply into metrics in a few pages, but, for now, understand this basic equation:

A greater number of *qualified* prospects into your system will always equal more clients on the other end, whether you get access to those clients yourself or through your partners. However you can, you need to get in front of as many people as you can and maximize your exposure through multiple marketing channels in order to create a successful launch.

That's where your marketing plan comes in and, with it, a sales plan to help you translate eyeballs into revenue.

In fact, your marketing and sales plan is so important to your launch that it gets its own section.

Your One-Two Punch: Marketing & Sales

We love marketing and sales. At its heart, it's a simple process: attract the attention of qualified prospective clients, build a relationship with them and convert them into paying clients. We also delight in how powerful the fundamentals of marketing are on their own. Grasp a few simple concepts and you, too can reap the rewards.

Where your product launch is concerned, your marketing and sales plan should do three things:

1. Maximize the channels available to you to bring as many *qualified* prospects into your system as possible.

2. Establish a relationship by delivering value up front.

3. Convert these prospects into paying clients.

Let's break it down even more specifically:

1. **Maximize Your Marketing Channels**

   In basic terms, maximizing your channels boils down to this: communicating with potential prospects through as many venues as possible, such as:

   - One-on-one (in person)
   - Webinars or Teleseminars
   - Email
   - Video marketing
   - Affiliates & joint ventures
   - Advertising (online and offline)
   - Media & Public relations
   - Live Events (seminars, local meeting groups)
   - Social media
   - Networking (online and offline)
   - Content marketing
   - Mobile marketing
   - And the list goes on…

Reaching people through multiple channels allows you to cast a wider net. Just as we discussed that people have preferred modalities for learning, people also have preferred ways of receiving marketing messages. For example, if you sent Pam a video, she'd probably skip it. However, she might be willing to read a piece of content you posted to Facebook or if it came through a referral source she trusted.

Multi-channel marketing also keeps you from putting all your eggs in one basket. It's your Plan B, C and D in case Plan A doesn't quite go the way you hoped.

As you form your product launch plan, stay open to channels you may not have tried before. Even though blogs and social media may not always seem like direct revenue generators, recent statistics offer a different take. 57% of businesses surveyed by Hubspot have acquired a customer through a company blog and 42% acquired a customer through Twitter.[31]

That's why your marketing plan should address utilizing as many of these channels as possible—*as appropriate to your ideal client.* While you do want to get your message in front of as many people as possible, remember that your goal isn't to attract just anybody.

Your goal is to attract your ideal match. Then, once you've attracted them into your system, you'll want to…

2. **Build Relationships with Your Prospects**

    Ideally your marketing system will capture the contact information of every prospect who inquires about what you've got to offer. Most people do this by offering value-added content in exchange for contact information, usually an email address in a process called an opt-in.

---

31   http://blog.hubspot.com/blog/tabid/6307/bid/11414/12-Mind-Blowing-Statistics-Every-Marketer-Should-Know.aspx

This is vital to your success because it opens up a new channel: email communication. Once you have captured someone's email, you can share additional marketing messages with them with the click of your mouse.

But you don't want to share just any messages with them. You want to add value up front and ask for nothing in return.

This might take the form of a video series, the first several of which have zero sales messages in them. They're just pure content to give your prospect a taste of who you are and what you can deliver. It might be a white paper. It might be a mobile application to download. Giving away a digital or physical book is another powerful strategy. The possibilities are limitless and depend heavily on 1) what your ideal client avatar wants and 2) how they are best influenced.

Whatever it is, know this: make it as *amazing* as you can. If you want to really get the attention of your prospects, you need to blow their minds for free. After all, so many things are available to us for free today:

- Wikipedia, a giant encyclopedia with 23 million+ articles: free.
- Facebook, our online social network and endless time sink: free.
- Hulu, on-demand television and movies: free.
- Craigslist, a place to get a job, sell your furniture, locate a place to live and even find love: free.

And those are just your legal options!

In other words, in a world where free is a given, value is tougher to establish. In order to grab mindshare in an increasingly noisy and devalued world, you'll have to create something that stands out.

You also need to be aware that building this relationship isn't a one-and-done process. You'll need to continue to add value—and you'll need to consciously...

3. **Convert These Prospects into Paying Clients**

In conventional marketing wisdom, experts used to say that it took 5-7 "touches" to convert a prospect to a buyer. That might still be true, but it varies heavily, depending on what you're selling and who you're selling it to. It might take as many as 20. It might take as few as two. It varies from product to product and person to person.

The point is: in the real world, most prospects will need to hear from you multiple times before they convert to buyers.

Your job is to provide them the opportunities to move down the marketing funnel and become clients.

This might take the form of a second (or third!) video in which you lay out the offer. It might be a direct marketing style email that directly asks a prospect to invest. It might be a pitch at the end of a content-filled webinar. Mike's favorite happens to be live webcasts, where he'll go live for anywhere from 4-12 hours, teaching concepts and explaining his offer. It might take a combination of all of t hese things.

Whatever sales activities you choose, keep in mind you have to ask for the sale. It's what will close the deal.

The Ultimate Ingredient for Your Launch

There's one final ingredient that's vital to a successful launch, and it's the glue that binds all of these ingredients together.

Every great launch is driven by a great story.

The story of your product is the heart of a launch. Your story answers the questions: "Why this? And why now?" It reveals your product as the ultimate solution to an incredibly relevant problem. It represents an opportunity that's the result of an incredibly fortuitous convergence of factors.

It explains why there's never been a better time to act than now. It also reveals to your potential clients, "Why you?"

Your product story unfolds your own personal journey, detailing how you got where you are today, to position you as the credible expert whose unique background positions you as the exact right person to lead your clients toward success.

Your product's story also captures all the emotions of possibility—of transformation, of excitement, of joy, of intrigue. It serves them up into a heady cocktail, resulting in the rapt attention of your prospects.

A story gives your product, and therefore its initial launch, meaning. It also gives your launch direction and provides your clients with the emotional impetus they need to commit—and invest with you.

Your product story is an incredibly important part of your launch. Embrace it and watch as it ties all the other ingredients together with a nice big bow.

Once you successfully combine all of the ingredients for a successful launch, there still remain two areas to watch out for. These challenges are ones that trip up even the most experienced marketers.

We'll tackle those next to help ensure smooth sailing for you.

Challenge #1: Metrics

Your car has a dashboard. On it you can see your speed, RPMs, gas level, oil levels and indicators that tell you if all your doors are closed or if any engine problems exist. On the surface, the car dashboard is deceptively simple and helps you understand at a glance how your car is working. It keeps you away from seeing "raw" engine data.

Every good business should have some kind of "dashboard" that shows how it's doing. It should include items like basic financial information, cost of goods, average sales, etc. These basic metrics are your guide for decision-making. They show you how to do more of what's working for you and less of what's not. This is especially critical during a product launch, in which you're trying to great results quickly.

Today, measuring your metrics is simple. If you have a Google Analytics account, they'll even serve them up in a dashboard. Most email programs do the same. It's easy to check your numbers regularly and focus your efforts on improving them.

As we said a few pages ago, marketing is a math problem. Metrics are the key to solving it. They'll help you pinpoint your exact challenge areas and show you where you need to take action. Metrics can open powerful pathways to success by helping you optimize your campaigns exactly where you need to.

Every now and then, we'll think that we're smart enough to operate on instincts. We'll say things like, "There's no way that this page could outperform that one." Even now, after 20+ years of experience each, sometimes the numbers still surprise us. That's why we're committed to, as our friend Mike Cline put it, being scientists.

Get in the habit of checking your numbers, testing new ideas, then discarding what doesn't work.

At a basic level, in terms of online marketing, here's what you should know:

- **Traffic:** How many people are seeing your page, your ad or your email?
- **Action Rate**: What percentage of those people are taking the action you want them to?
    - Clicking (Click-through rate)
    - Opening your email (Open rate)
    - Opting in (Opt-in rate)
    - Buying (Conversion rate)
- **Return on Investment:** For every output of marketing dollars, are you bringing in enough money to cover the expenses and, even better, turn a profit?

It's important to analyze each piece of data individually to understand exactly where your roadblocks lie. For example, let's say you send out an email with a link to buy your book. No one buys.

Why? Your metrics will tell the story:

- **What percentage of your list opened your email?** If it was unusually low, it's because of your subject line.

- **What percentage of your list clicked through to your page?** Low numbers here point to problems in your email copy.

- **What percentage who clicked through actually bought?** Low numbers here point to problems on your webpage or an unclear offer.

At this point in the process, many entrepreneurs come down with "Keeping up with the Joneses" syndrome again. They want to know what are "good" numbers and what are "bad" numbers. Objective numbers don't matter nearly as much as *progress* does.

When you're looking to build a relationship with your prospects, you want to see your numbers improve over time. That's how you judge how well you're doing. Comparing your numbers to someone else's may provide you a goal to aim for, but they won't tell you a story worth listening to.

But what if you're doing well, your list is responsive to your offers, but you're just not selling enough stuff to make ends meet?

When we hear that question, it usually points to challenge #2…

Challenge #2: The Traffic Conundrum

A lot of times, what people think is a conversion problem, isn't.

The problem is not getting enough eyeballs on your offer.

Think of it this way: good conversion rates in the Internet marketing world hover around 1-2%. That means for every 100 people who visit your page, you can hope two of those people will buy your offer on a good day.

If you want to close more than two people a day, you need to get more than 100 people to your page every day. It's a simple solution: more sales relies on more traffic. And let's be clear: it's got to be *qualified* traffic, people who are close to your ideal client avatar.

There are many ways to bring traffic to your site. The most common include:

1. **Organic traffic** from unpaid search results, press releases, blogs, articles and videos.

2. **Paid traffic** from things like online cost-per-click advertising where you're paying for placement.

3. **Joint venture traffic** from customers of your partners and affiliates.

4. **Offline traffic** from television, radio interviews and other more traditional sources.

Of these, joint venture traffic is probably the most unpredictable—with potential for explosive results—and expensive ones.

Here's why:

Usually, when you're partnering with someone through a joint venture or affiliate agreement, you've offered them a cut of your revenue that might start as low as 20% and go all the way up to 50%.

And most times, this cut comes out of your gross revenue before you've taken out expenses. So, if you're selling a $1,000 product with a 40% commission, your affiliate will receive $400. If it's going to cost you $200 to make it, you'll also walk away with $400. You put in all the work of creating, producing and packaging the product and the two of you might walk away with the same revenue per sale.

However, if you're matched up with the right partner, he or she can have the potential to double, triple or even quadruple your traffic. It can be a tough call, one you'll have to make on a case-by-case basis.

With any traffic source, you should be examining your return on investment on each. In other words, how much does it cost to get a new customer? For an affiliate, there's a pretty straightforward answer: your cost per customer equals your commission.

For paid traffic, the calculation becomes a little more complex, but still fairly straightforward. Let's look at our previous example conversion rate of 2%. If it costs you $2 per click to get those 100 people to your page, then your cost per customer equals:

$$\frac{\text{Cost per 100 clicks}}{\text{Conversion percentage}} \quad \frac{\$200}{2} = \$100 \text{ per customer}$$

Now, look at the margin on your product. Are you making enough to justify paying $100 per customer? If not, you'll want to rethink your paid strategy.

For organic traffic, you'll want to consider the costs of any search optimization work you've done. You'll need to pick a time period for analysis. If you started your SEO work in March, you might consider the period from March 1–April 30 and calculate your numbers for that time period. Your formula will be:

$$\frac{\text{SEO Optimization Cost}}{\text{Number of conversions}} \quad \frac{\$500}{10} = \$50 \text{ per customer}$$

One final consideration: Even though some forms of traffic will be cheaper than others, we recommend you pursue a mix. Why? Google algorithms change. Relationships shift. CPC ads lose effectiveness. Employing a variety of methods ensures that no one change will wipe out your entire traffic stream, which could set you back *months*.

One Final Distinction

We've spent this chapter showing you how to create an effective launch and brings its benefits to bear on your business. Before we close, we want to remind you of one more thing.

Your initial product launch will not make or break your business. Your long-term marketing plan *will*.

That's why you need to get serious about 1) evergreen product delivery systems and 2) long-term marketing systems.

These two things will create consistent streams of revenue and help you create the Make, Market, Launch IT business of your dreams. They'll provide you enough cash flow to keep your doors open, your contractors paid and your lifestyle funded. They're your security blanket, the consistency that lets you sleep at night.

As we said at the outset, we're committed to helping you build a real business around your product. These two distinctions will help you do just that.

Evergreen Product Delivery

After your initial launch, you have options for what you want to do with your product.

Some people who have used urgency and scarcity tactics within their launch formula close their carts and put their product on the shelf for a year. It's a great technique for closing sales, but it can shorten your product's lifecycle. When you bring it out again, will it still be relevant? Will people still want it? Or will it feel past its prime?

The overarching question becomes this:

Could you have gotten it in more people's hands—and maximized your revenue for this version of your product—by making it available in some form throughout the year?

If you believe the answer is yes, then consider setting up an evergreen version of your product for delivery.

Your Business Lifeline: a Long-Term Marketing Plan

The long-term success of your business starts here, with a long-term revenue plan that focuses on attracting prospects and turning them into buyers.

Creating a marketing plan ensures that you'll know what to do and when—no matter how busy you get. It will also keep a consistent stream of new prospects coming into your funnel, prospects who your sales system will turn into buyers. This constant flow of prospects is key to a consistent flow of revenue that will keep your business afloat throughout its first year and the many years to come.

As you create your marketing plan, make sure it supports three major goals in your business:

1. Growing your list of prospects.
2. Promoting and selling your products to these prospects.
3. Building and protecting your brand.

The most important thing is to do all three of these things consistently. Even small, consistent actions add up to more than occasional, frenetic activity. That's why you need to sit down and make a plan for at least the next six months.

Stripped down to its basics, a marketing plan can be as simple as:

1. Identifying your top-level goals for your business, either using the above list or creating your own.
2. Defining where you are and where you want to be in what period of time.
3. Brainstorming the steps to get you there.
4. Making final decisions and put dates on them.
5. Measuring as you go to determine what works and what doesn't.

We suggest sitting down once a year to construct an overall plan for the next 12 months, then carving out time every quarter to evaluate the effectiveness of your strategies (using the metrics we discussed earlier!) and tweaking as necessary.

Final Thoughts

Although the title of this chapter focuses on your launch, it's about more than that. It's about setting up the sales and marketing systems that create a real business around your product, a business that brings in a consistent stream of revenue to support your lifestyle goals.

When you can create the atmosphere of success by building the systems that support it and the plan that keeps it on track, you'll be on your way to creating something special.

In fact, that's what Mary Poul had in mind when she created her Sales Mastery Summit. As she began work on her primary product, she realized that she needed a way to continually build a list to market it to. The Sales Mastery Summit was born and, she soon had a list of 11,000 potential customers—and growing. See how she did it in the following case study.

 **"I built a list of 11,000 viewers in 4 Weeks."**
Case Study from the Field: Mary Poul

It's one thing to build a product. It's quite another to build a following. But that's exactly what Mary Poul did after going through Make, Market, Launch IT.

After her previous employer decided not to act on an idea she'd created, Mary seized the opportunity. She created *Bankable Business Value*, an information product that helps strategic account reps get and grow important accounts with a co-designed value delivery plan. However, as she worked on the product, she knew there was something missing.

After starting Make, Market, Launch IT, it hit her: she needed an escalation plan.

As Mary explains: "There was always something telling me, I'm missing something here, and an 'aha' came through Make, Market, Launch IT—I didn't have a 'what comes next.' I didn't have any kind of escalation built around my product to make it really worth the effort to launch. So I mapped out a business model that would make the product worth launching."

Mary honed in on her target audience—high-end sales professionals and strategic account managers. After evaluating their needs, she decided to create an online event to draw them in. She called it the *Sales Mastery Summit* and featured top sales experts who shared their "best-of-the-best" strategies with Mary in an interview format.

The idea took off.

After launching her first *Sales Mastery Summit*, Mary added over 11,000 followers to her list in less than two months.

By setting up her experts as affiliates, she was able to leverage these relationships to promote the summit. Most of the experts reacted favorably to this arrangement. "Nobody was squeamish," she says—with one exception. One well-connected expert had agreed to the interview, but didn't want to promote it to her list. However, Mary's interview style won her over. "At the end of the interview, she said, 'I really like what you're building, I'm going to go ahead and promote it for you,'" Mary recalls.

The fact that Mary presented herself as a reporter—rather than a competing expert—helped her build these relationships easily. "Since I'm not presenting myself as an expert, I'm very non-threatening to them. It's not as if I'm trying to take over their client base or anything. It was just an overall smart way to build my network in a space that I don't work in," Mary says.

It also gave her a strong network for the future. "With all of the experts I'm now networked with, I've got a nice partner network to help me in whatever I want to launch in that space," she says.

In addition to affiliate relationships, Mary also credits Make, Market, Launch IT's offer-building process for the success of the Sales Mastery Summit. "Really thinking through the offer was so helpful—and what's going to attract somebody into it," she said. For the summit, that meant allowing people to tune in for free on the day of the broadcast and charging for upgraded access.

Make, Market, Launch IT also helped Mary expand her possibilities. As she was developing her offer, Mary realized there were others who could benefit from her services as well. She decided to expand into a new niche.

"I started out really targeting sales professionals as the niche because that really is the client base for most of the experts," she explains. "However, I quickly realized that the appeal was much broader. Small business owners also want to be able to upgrade their sales skills and have so little time to do it since they have a lot of hats to wear. This is a nice format for them."

Mary is now in the process of going back through the Make, Market, Launch IT process to craft a marketing plan to reach this new audience. She is also planning to test a few additional components she can add to her sales funnel and product offer for next year.

As she continues her own product development, Mary has complemented these activities with consulting services. Mary has begun working with consultants to help maximize their business revenue. One client, she says, "does a bang-up job in his keynotes and consulting, but didn't build a list, in spite of talking to over 50,000 people each year. And he didn't have anything to offer after a presentation, no back-of-the-room products." That's where Mary—and the Make, Market, Launch IT framework—comes in.

Finally, Mary credits Make, Market, Launch IT for being the final polish on her package. "I got the education that I needed so that I could actually deliver something that was going to succeed," she says. She finished the program with the "confidence to just go for it and know that I…would really provide value to the viewer so it was worth their time to tune in."

Mary Poul launches *Bankable Business Value* in May 2013. She continues to expand the Sales Mastery Summit at **SalesMasterySummit.com**.

Step 7: Grow
Build Your Power Tribe
& Scale Your Business

Once you set the foundation for the revenue-generating activities that will fund your business, the final step in your Make, Market, Launch IT business will set up a catalyst for growth to maintain your long-term health and success.

The catalyst we have in mind has long been a fundamental principle for building any sustainable business. And, as we said earlier, you simply can't run this business alone. **You need to create strong long-term relationships with your customers.**

But in order to make this strategy a true catalyst for growth, we invite you to take it a step further. We encourage you to invest in something greater, something that will contribute significantly to the expansion of your business—geometrically.

We're talking about creating your very own Power Tribe.

Product creation is a marathon, not a sprint. Along this journey, you're looking for people to run with you, ideally for the entire course. But what if instead of being mere running buddies, these people could recruit more runners along the journey? Instead of completing a long, solo journey, you'll be in the middle of a fun, high-achieving group of athletes who keep you running—*and keep each other going* by inspiring the whole group at every mile.

That's the clout of a Power Tribe.

A Power Tribe, as we see it, is a self-sufficient community of raving fan, high-compliance customers who will:

1. **Support your mission** because it's something they believe in, too.

2. **Extend your impact** by sharing your ideas with their friends, family and colleagues.

3. **Create a consistent stream of referrals** by bringing other people into the Tribe.

4. **Help others achieve** the success they've experienced by working within the community.

Rarely, if ever, do these Power Tribes form by accident. They're created, fostered and nurtured.

As the Internet makes our shopping experiences ever more impersonal, there's tremendous opportunity for you to step in and rally people. When you present yourself authentically, proudly sharing your unique blend of expertise and perspective, you'll will draw people toward you, simply for the virtue of being different and being *real*.

We mentioned earlier that product creation is not about being everything to everybody. **Creating your Power Tribe is about being everything to somebody.** It's about taking a stand for what you believe in and creating a place for people with similar beliefs.

Creating your Power Tribe is about starting a movement with your product—or your brand—at the center.

When you're forming a Power Tribe, you're using a completely different model of communication. You're not shouting to the masses. Instead, you're having a quiet conversation with a few, select people who are hanging on your every word.

Power Tribes represent an opportunity to get your voice heard—and to get people truly invested in what you do.

Forming a Power Tribe is about *investing* in your niche's passions and their success.

What do they love? What do they hate? What has contributed to their success with your products and services?

Have you ever seen two Jeep owners wave at each other as they pass? It's called the Jeep Wave, and it's Jeep owners' protocol that's even been included in the official owner's manual. The wave was cleverly defined as "an honor bestowed upon those drivers with the superior intelligence, taste, class and discomfort tolerance to own the ultimate vehicle— the Jeep. Generally consists of vigorous side-to-side motion of one or both hands, but may be modified to suit circumstances and locally accepted etiquette."[32]

As they hit their 70th anniversary, Jeep leveraged this tradition to create a sense of pride in its owners, foster community spirit[33] and— hopefully—to create new or repeat Jeep owners. If you need evidence of the power of this Tribe, you can see its motto: "It's a Jeep thing. You wouldn't understand" on bumper stickers, t-shirts and every other kind of merchandise you can imagine.

To create your own tribe, you need to understand what drives them wild with desire, what has led to their success and shine a light on it. Once they're all stirred up, it's a matter of giving them a platform to communicate on, a series of rituals or a community to participate in.

---

32 http://jeeptalk.org/jeep_wave.php
33 http://blog.jeep.com/2010/12/29/long-live-the-jeep%C2%AE-wave/

The Magic of Power Tribes

Often, tribes are formed for practical reasons. For example, no hunter can eat a whole deer by himself in one sitting. Tribes create an efficient way to share resources, exchange knowledge, band together against the enemy for protection and continue the line of existence by sparking marriages and offspring.

But there's something magical about tribes when they really come together. You can't put a price on a sense of community. You also can't predict the amazing feats that you can accomplish when you're supported by a group of family and friends.

In other words, Tribes create something greater than the individual sum of its parts.

And although you may already have an idea of what a Power Tribe can do for your business, you might be surprised by some of the benefits.

Your Power Tribe will act as an extension of your sales force.

When you are not only meeting—but also feeding into—a person's deep desires, the result is fanaticism around your product. These customers will become life-long clients, the people who set you up for life.

Because they've already been successful using your product, they will not only buy all of your other products, but they'll also tell all their friends about you.

We tend to forget how powerful word-of-mouth marketing is, but what's more powerful than a recommendation from a friend? Nothing, according to a recent survey, which clocks "Word of Mouth" as the biggest influencer in a purchasing decision, beating out web research and online reviews.[34]

When you add a new member to your Power Tribe, you're essentially expanding your sales force—for free.

---

34 http://www.pr-squared.com/index.php/2011/11/the-power-of-word-of-mouth-marketing-infographic-edition

Your Power Tribe will grow your business—and not just in revenue alone.

After they buy all your products, your Power Tribe will demand more—more products and higher levels of service. They'll want the advanced version and the platinum version, along with a coaching package.

Listen to your Power Tribe, and they will also feed you ideas for what they need. Inventing your next product can be as simple as filling the next gaping hole in their lives.

Remember, long-term success comes from the constant escalation of your offers to your customers. Having a group of highly successful, long-term customers will push you to create new, higher-end products and services that advance your message even further.

Your Power Tribe will help you build a legacy, not just a product.

People want to belong to something that they believe in. Renowned psychologist Abraham Maslow named "belonging" as one of his five basic human needs.[35] People yearn for community, a place where they matter. If you can gather a tribe and build them a community, a close-knit group who knows each others' names and misses each other when they're gone, people will love you for it.

You'll become much more to them than a business contact. You'll become their hero.

And, the impact of your business, your mission and your legacy will start to grow virally—literally creating a life of its own.

It All Starts with Your Mission

Creating your Power Tribe begins here, with the values you believe in as an entrepreneur and as a person. These values drive everything you do: your product creation, your marketing and even the setup of your business.

---

35 http://en.wikipedia.org/wiki/Maslow%27s_hierarchy_of_needs

At the end of the day, what do you stand for? What's your mission?

What matters to you? At the end of your journey, what do you hope to leave behind?

The two of us share the burning desire to help people become entrepreneurs, to start their own businesses, become their own bosses, design products that align with their passions and enjoy lifestyles of their own design. It's been a heady, exciting journey for us and we love passing it on to other people, then watching them grow.

Have you been exploring and defining your mission as we've gone through this book together? If you need any inspiration, flip through this book and revisit the heroes of our case studies. We're proud to have such a diverse group, with each member pursuing his or her individual intersection of passion, expertise and values.

Whatever your overall mission becomes, grab onto it and live by it. It will create the basis by which you'll draw your Power Tribe to you. You also might want to ask yourself this question: At the end of your entrepreneurial journey, what do you hope to leave behind?

It's a philosophy, one that we certainly didn't invent, but one we wholeheartedly embrace:

Our customers come first.

Think about how well that gels with our mission. Our whole reason for existence is to support budding entrepreneurs—our customers—and help them realize their vision. Of course they come first.

If your mission can't support this philosophy, or you simply don't agree with it, that's okay. We'd never tell you what to believe. However, a Power Tribe simply won't work for you. Customers need to be the focal point of your business, the heroes of your brand story, in order for you to create a community around them.

If you do embrace this philosophy, the benefits are tremendous. And sometimes unexpected.

Power Tribes in Action

One of the most famous and recognizable Power Tribes out there today belongs to Apple. Those people standing outside in the rain for the next iPad, iPhone or iGadget? That's Apple's Power Tribe in action.

There are many other brands out there fostering their relationships with their customers and creating Power Tribes on their own scale. We offer you two examples as added inspiration:

New Belgium Brewery

Smaller craft breweries like Colorado-based New Belgium have to compete with the advertising and marketing power of large companies like MillerCoors and Anheuser-Busch for market share. Their weapon? An army of devotees. New Belgium's Power Tribe is made up of customers who will go to great lengths to seek out their beers, aided by a search engine on the New Belgium website and a mobile application.

To foster its Power Tribe, New Belgium has taken it a step further. Riffing on the branding of its popular bicycle logo and its premier brew, Fat Tire, **the company founded a movement called Team Wonderbike.** Its mission:

"Currently more than 20,000 strong, we on Team Wonderbike have pledged to bike—not drive—better than 14 million miles in the coming year. But that's just the beginning. We need you (and your family and friends too) to take the pledge and commit to biking whenever you can. We're building an online community with regional chapters and a national voice for sensible transportation alternatives. And we're having a damn good time doing it."

Devotees can log bike trips on the New Belgium website, as well as pledge future miles and view biking maps from other users. Given that the craft brewing demographic is full of "adventurous" Millenials[36] who may be more open to alternative transport, this cause is likely right up their alley.

When you can reach for any beer, wouldn't you reach for one that supports—and fosters—a cause you believe in?

Read more about the brewery at **NewBelgium.com**. (And the beer's pretty good, too!)

AMC

In order to channel—and nurture—the fanatical devotion to its popular television shows like *Breaking Bad, Mad Men* and the *Walking Dead*, AMC.com has created a hub of interactivity. Fans can take quizzes to earn badges, participate in discussion boards, watch behind-the-scenes videos and digitally insert their own faces into scenes from shows, allowing them to temporarily "star" in their favorite series.

They've also created extensions of their popular characters, publishing blogs "written" by *Breaking Bad*'s Marie and websites advertising the services of *Breaking Bad*'s ambulance-chasing lawyer, Saul Goodman. These fun features **allow fans to deepen their relationships with the characters they love** by interacting with them.

AMC has even extended into mobile technology, creating a classic cocktail app that fans of *Mad Men* can download in order to drink like Don Draper. *Walking Dead* fans can play their own adventure game on the go.

In short, AMC knows how to stoke the fires of its fans.

Explore the full roster of fan resources at **AMC.com**.

36 http://www.beveragemedia.com/index.php/2012/05/who-is-the-new-beer-consumer-brewers-ready-to-say-ihola-and-more-to-expand-reach/

Assembling Your Power Tribe

How can you create a Power Tribe in your own business to support your mission and spark long-term growth? It starts with…

Catalyst #1: Identify Heroes Early On

Heroes are the people who can rally your tribe, who can become leaders within your community and will, in turn, nurture others to create similar success. By now, you've met some of our heroes through the case studies in this book. We met most of them through our Facebook Community, which we established to give Make, Market, Launch IT members a place to talk amongst themselves.

That's the second item you'll need to foster your Power Tribe…

Catalyst #2: Create a Platform for Interaction

Creating this community involved some up-front work for us, including making it easy for people to find and enticing to join. We also had to make sure that it was a protected place, one accessible only to our customers. By restricting entry to customers, we were able to safeguard everyone's time. We knew everyone who joined the group had invested in the same business goals. There wouldn't be trolls to taunt anyone or time-wasting tourists who were just there for the free stuff.

Before long—in fact, quickly enough to surprise us—people were introducing themselves in the community and tossing around ideas. Some members posted their opt-in pages and asked for feedback. Some posted inspiration for others who might be struggling. Some confessed their challenges. The Make, Market, Launch IT Facebook community has become an incredibly valuable place to get advice—and give back.

Through that community, people began to report early successes. These people were often the same people who were active within the community, who were quick to offer a word of advice or a resource to another person experiencing a challenge.

Those are kinds of people who will become your heroes, people who are:

- **Successful**—Customers who have produced a substantiated high-level result by using your product or service.

- **Relatable**—Heroes who match your core avatars and who other customers will relate to and aspire to be.

- **Contribution-Oriented**—The type of people who value giving back and helping others succeed.

- **Mission-Oriented**—People who share your company's values and believe in the mission behind what you're doing as a business.

Ultimately, just as you will help your customers grow through their journey with you, you'll help your heroes grow as well. You'll help them escalate their experience.

That process forms the next catalyst for creating your Power Tribe.

 Your House, Your Rules

When you establish your community, make sure to set ground rules. That doesn't mean censoring people who don't share your point of view. It means standing up as the leader of your tribe and letting your followers know what's okay and what's not.

You may choose to create a very loose set of rules, such as: "Tell the truth. Be nice." Or you may create a more specific set of ground rules. Ask yourself: what are your expectations for your community? What do you require from your customers to participate?

Whatever set of rules you choose, make them public, easy to find and clear to understand. When those rules are violated, you *must* step in and remove the offending members. As its leader, your tribe is counting on you.

A Note About Honesty

We want to see the good in people and we hope you do, too.

However, there are some cases in which it serves you to be skeptical, and this can be one of them.

This may come in the form of canceled checks, order receipts or whatever it takes.

Why? We're sorry to say that we've been burned in the past by people who were so desperate for the spotlight that they ended up inflating their claims.

It's embarrassing for them and it's embarrassing for you. If there's any possibility that you could have known about the dishonesty, it can also get you into legal trouble.

Do yourself a favor: be optimistic, but skeptical of everyone who comes through your door. Make it a standing policy to provide proof before you feature anyone, no exceptions. That way, you won't risk offending any particular person.

A policy like this will save you lots of heartache in the long run and protect your reputation from a potential disaster.

Catalyst #3: Escalate Your Heroes

It's the ultimate gift you can give someone: to bring them to a level that they may never have even considered for themselves. As you build your business—and your Power Tribe around it—you'll also want to escalate your customers and support their progress through four levels:

1. **Hero**

    Your model customers will become your heroes, an integral part of your marketing. Give them the opportunity to share their results and experiences, and use their testimonials as social proof. You'll need to coach them on how to most effectively tell their stories of transformation to create a stark "before and after." Use these stories to help prospects overcome buying objections, and ultimately trigger a buying decision.

2. **Teacher**

The most communicative heroes can evolve to become teachers. Being taught by somebody "just like you" can be far more powerful than learning the material from someone much farther along. Using former customers as teachers will make the possibility of results seem that much more attainable.

3. **Promoter**

Next, your teachers can also become promoters on behalf of your business. At this stage, your heroes may begin to see enormous profits as well, which will support them in their lives and potentially build their careers.

4. **Partner**

The final and most exciting part of the hero escalation pathway is when somebody who began as a customer becomes a business partner. You can give your best promoters the gift of the platform, and eventually give them the opportunity to coach, teach and find prospects for their personal business while marketing your products.

This process begins with you: with identifying your heroes early on, recognizing them, then offering them a platform to communicate. It might be within your online community, or you might do as we have: feature them in a book, an online webcast, or in our newsletter. Allow them to be visible within your community and let them speak for themselves to guide others.

You'll also want to remember to check in with your heroes periodically and nurture them as they grow. As they shape your business, this mentoring will be your way of giving back.

Now that you've established a community with the help of your heroes to guide it, you'll need to start translating community success into financial success.

Catalyst #4: Continue to Make Offers

Even as you bask in the warmth of creating a community and fostering the heroes within it, you need to keep your original goals in mind.

If you want your Power Tribe to be a true catalyst for business growth, you need to remember to do one thing: continue to offer your community ways to invest with you through offers at varying price points.

In other words, if you want your customers to continue to buy from you, you need to continue to give them that opportunity. If you've built a powerful community, they'll probably be clamoring for them as it is. These could be opportunities that you've created for them to escalate their success. It could be offers from your launch partners that add value to your customers' lives.

You'll want to remember to balance these opportunities for investment with the value-added content. In these long-term relationships, there's *give* as well as *take*. If you focus on our original goals, to continue to 1) add value and 2) create success, you'll have no trouble walking that line.

You'll also want to take it one step further.

Catalyst #5: Reward Your Customers' Loyalty

The value of the warm fuzzies generated by loyalty perks can't be calculated—and it shouldn't be underestimated when creating a Power Tribe to sustain your business.

Think of the feeling you've gotten if you've ever heard your name called for a free upgrade to First Class, received a free cup of coffee after buying 10 cups from your local shop or received a $20 coupon in the mail after buying a few pairs of shoes from DSW.

There's delight. There's joy. There's also pride, all of which make you want to continue to buy from these brands.

One of the easiest form of loyalty rewards comes in the form of repeat buyer discounts. In fact, we always make sure that our previous customers get the best possible price on any future offerings we create.

We assemble a whole separate set of communications specifically aimed toward them, to make sure they feel cared for at the highest level.

While loyalty can be rewarded with a discount, we encourage you to get creative. What else could you offer your customers?

Can you offer customers access to your product a week before it's released? Early access has an exclusive, insiders' feel to it.

If you can involve a sense of ritual, even better. There's power in consistency. For example, can you broadcast a yearly webcast that's only available to paying customers?

As you consider the possibilities, think of the emotions you can create: excitement, surprise, delight, importance, belonging. By tapping into these, you'll create an even more powerful experience.

Finally, you'll need one more element to complete your Power Tribe: and it comes from within you.

Catalyst #6: Be a Beacon

We started this chapter by discussing our mission and asking you about yours. The final thing that binds a Power Tribe together is their belief system.

You need to give your Tribe something to believe in.

This belief is already there, inside of you. Let it shine through in everything you do. Just as it drives you personally, let it drive you publicly.

Your customers are looking to you for inspiration as much as they're looking to you for solutions.

What does your product mean to you? What does your business mean to you? Make these forces a part of your product and a part of your communications. As you stand up for what you believe in, you'll stand out.

Do it for you and do it for your Tribe.

As you do, you'll step into the real role you've created: entrepreneur, product creator, visionary and leader.

To fill this role, you need to set up your business to support the people that will get you there in the first place: your customers.

Creating Raving Fan Customers

Long-term customer relationships are the key to a thriving business. Think back to the Cycle of Transformation that we introduced in Chapter 1. When you create success, it starts a waterfall effect, drawing in repeat customers who believe in you, as well as new and referral customers they've recruited.

But if you can't keep customers past a single cycle or two, you're going to have to work a lot harder to find new customers. In fact, a study by Forrester Research revealed that it can cost five times as much to acquire a customer than to satisfy and retain a current customer.[37]

That's why it's so important to set up your business to support your customers so they can, in turn, support your business. It begins with establishing policies and procedures at every level to ensure that your customers are cared for—before you make your first sale. As companies like Zappos have so famously done, put them in writing and make sure they're clearly communicated to every member of your staff, including any contractors. Include both your overarching, big ideas as well as the nitty-gritty policies that drive your customer interactions.

When creating your systems, we highly recommend modeling organizations you respect. When you have a good experience as a customer, ask yourself how you can repeat this experience for your own customers.

---

37   http://www.destinationcrm.com/Articles/Web-Exclusives/Viewpoints/Listen-to-the-Voice-of-the-Customer-53239.aspx

For example, we love how empowered Zappos staff is to fix any problems they encounter. We had a recent experience in which a marketing email promised us access to Zappos VIP program, but, when clicked, the link turned out to be incorrect. The first person who responded (within an hour) had both apologized and granted us access to the program with no further action required on our part. It won us over and created more goodwill than if the email had simply worked the first time.

That's why we see customer service problems as *opportunities.* Customers who don't care, don't complain. When someone calls up to give your staff an earful, it's because they have a lot invested in your product, either financially, emotionally or psychologically, and they want to keep working with you.

If you handle the situation right, it's entirely possible to turn upset into an equal and opposite amount of satisfaction—and relief.

The truth is, so many times, people just want to be *heard.* They want to know that someone is listening to their problems—and that the other person cares.

That's why we train our staff to meet the customer where he or she is. We train them that our policies aren't more important than our customers. And, ultimately, we tell them that it doesn't matter who's wrong and who's right.

What matters is getting the customers' problems solved quickly, in a way that supports them and our ongoing business. We set clear expectations as to when customers can expect a resolution and keep them updated on the progress. We also ask ourselves and our staff how we can prevent these problems in the future.

Truth be told, most of the time, people are simply gratified to receive a human response to their problems. That serves 95% of them. The other 5% may require some extra attention from our staff, but we're happy to do it.

In fact, we're *thrilled* to do it. Happy customers mean long-term customers and a strong future for our business.

But besides that, happy customers make us *happy*. They melt our hearts with their kind emails. They inspire us with their stories. In fact, happy customers represent some of our greatest triumphs. Take these tools and use them to create your own victories. The joy—and the benefits—of clients well satisfied is waiting for you.

Of course, in order to have the energy to create these satisfied clients, you need to support one more super-important person: yourself.

The Psychology of the Long-Term Entrepreneur

If you're anything like us, you're the last person you take care of.

As you've seen in this chapter, we're obsessed with taking impeccable care of our customers. We're also incredibly committed to taking care of our staff and contractors because we're so grateful for all that they enable us to do. On the personal side, both of us have embraced the entrepreneurial lifestyle to make sure we have the time for our partners and our children.

In order to take care of all of these people, both emotionally and financially with your business, you need to take care of yourself.

Looking after yourself starts with creating the lifestyle that supports you.

For the two of us, that means not being chained to a desk, a cubicle or a boardroom all day. It means working out of coffee shops, out of our cars, out of home offices—anywhere we can access our phone, laptop and the Internet.

The flip side is this: as an entrepreneur, sometimes it's hard to switch off.

With our encouragement, get away from the day-to-day running of your business. Spend quality time with your customers and listen to their success stories, ones that you helped create! Give yourself the gift of hearing the impact you've had on other people's lives.

Draw boundaries of your own, both in your day-to-day life and by carving out time for your favorite hobby or whatever it is that recharges your batteries.

In other words, make sure to enjoy the fruits of your labor. Take the kids to Hawaii. Go hiking, or camping or whatever you enjoy. Let your brain slow down. Relax and enjoy. Spend some of that hard-earned money. You deserve it.

You'll return a happier, more focused entrepreneur, which will allow you to embrace the next piece of psychology we offer:

Be present.

It's so easy to divide your energy into little pieces and half-focus on everything, personally and professionally. If you've ever tried to admire a piece of your son's artwork while listening to a conference call and checking whether an email you've been waiting for has arrived, you know what we mean.

We love the pace of entrepreneurial life. It's what gives us fire. It's what makes it fun. But even as you move from task to task, we recommend devoting 100% of your energy to whatever you're doing, one thing at a time.

And stay in the present as much as you can. It's important to focus on the here and now. Don't dwell too much on what happened yesterday and don't get tunnel vision over the future. Take the actions that you can take *now*, to move your vision forward today.

Of course, you should absolutely take time to think about the future.

If there's a common thread we see running through the most successful entrepreneurs, it's that they're always keeping their pulse on what's next.

In other words, keep learning.

Do it in whatever way excites you. If you're a reader, splurge on an Amazon.com order and keep a stack on your bedside table or fill your Kindle with recommendations from friends and colleagues. Get your favorite blogs and news websites in one spot through an RSS feed and monitor it daily for articles that pique your interest.

Join a community to generate new and interesting ideas. Some colleagues have had great success with local Rotary clubs. Others have found their stride by participating in mastermind groups. Expose yourself to new people and new ideas. If you move beyond your usual haunts, you'll enable yourself to cross-pollinate your business with ideas from other disciplines.

Jump at the chance to speak. The fastest way to learn is to commit to speaking. It forces you to create new content. It also motivates you to keep learning for the sole purpose of teaching later on. Putting this kind of pressure on yourself is healthy. It forces you to get out of your comfort zone and grow. And remember, you just might be introduced to the biggest business opportunity of your life through a speaking engagement. You never know who will be in the audience.

Communicate with your customers. We can't tell you how many lessons we've learned from the people we're serving. Check in with your support staff and see what themes are emerging. Hold a Q&A webinar and see what people want to know.

There are sources for learning all around you. Part of the beauty of being an entrepreneur lies in being able to take advantage of these trends much faster than large companies, who run their decisions through a long chain of executives.

That's why we'll always encourage you to…

Be nimble.

Especially when you're leveraging online technology, it's possible to capitalize quickly on new ideas. Use this to your advantage as much as possible.

Being nimble also means being flexible. Unlike the giant grinding gears of a large corporation, your light and fast operations should be able to make a needed turn, if warranted. Think of your operation like a sports car. You can hit the gas quickly. You can maneuver around the field of slower cars. And, if needed, you can make a sharp right turn and go in a new direction. The right—and the power—is yours as an entrepreneur.

Wield it wisely and you'll be crossing the finish line in no time.

Wrapping It All Up: Three Master Lessons

In this book, we've given you a comprehensive set of tools and industry secrets to creating a product out of the intersection of your expertise, passion and a long-term successful business. We're so pleased to have made this journey with you, and we hope it's the first of many.

But true to its name, if there's anything you should take away from Make, Market, Launch IT it's these three core skills:

Make: How to create a polished product efficiently and with the fewest number of resources that solves the pain of your target audience in the form of an impeccably executed and packaged product.

Market: How to master the art of creating offers that your audience can't wait to invest in.

Launch: How to get your product out there in a big way and, at the same time, find your best customers: the people who get the best results, cause you the least stress and become life-long customers.

As we near the end of our journey, we offer you one final story from the field. Colin Hiles, a longtime blogger and established training specialist, saw Make, Market, Launch IT as his chance to leverage both his time—and the following he'd created with his website—to create a whole new revenue stream for himself.

 **"The end result will not be an hour's work for an hour's pay."**
Case Study from the Field: Colin Hiles

Colin Hiles has been blogging since 2009, not because he wanted to build a following and not because he had anything he wanted to sell. Colin was blogging simply because he enjoyed it.

With an established career as a training and development specialist in both corporate and sports environments, Colin never imagined he could turn his blog's ideas into anything more than a hobby—until he started getting emails about Make, Market, Launch IT.

Make, Market, Launch IT planted a seed. Colin started to think about creating a product around his belief system that he could sell to his existing blog followers. Around that same time, Colin also started getting queries from worldwide prospects asking him for a way to access his retreats, held mainly in Spain and Morocco, from other parts of the globe.

"That was perfect timing for me. It really got me thinking about [creating a product] seriously," Colin says. Make, Market, Launch IT gave Colin a two-pronged opportunity to turn both his blog and his 20 years of experience in mindset and belief training into products that he could leverage.

The solution seemed obvious. He decided to stop, in his words, "messing around" and to build two products, *Follow Your Smile* and *Mind Power+ Toolkit.*

To make sure he was on the right track, Colin started his product development in the Make, Market, Launch IT way: by understanding what his customers really need, then designing a product around those desires. "This was just following the process that Mike and Pam laid out. Get some feedback, find some needs, and then begin to address those needs," he says.

He started by reaching out to his existing community. "I sent an email out to my list and asked them to fill out the poll. So I took that and said, how do I help with [their biggest issues]: clarity, fear, and issues with money? And that's where the idea of Advanced Mind Power Training came up," he explains.

To test these ideas, he created a membership site called the Mind Power Academy and built his first product, The Mind Power + Toolkit. However, Colin decided to release it only to an exclusive group of people: his loyal followers. Only those who have been with him for the long haul were granted the opportunity to invest in his program—at least for now.

Since this group knows him well and trusts his work already, Colin used them as a testing ground to see what really sticks. By restricting access, he's also making his community part of the journey, which will ultimately keep them even more invested as he continues to expand his product line.

In other words, with his first product, Colin is already nurturing his Power Tribe. His initial launch brought 55 people into the program for beta testing.

Colin used the tools provided by Make, Market, Launch IT to set up his entire system, including his launch sequence, a membership site, four videos, a book, his products and all his branding. "Everything you see on my site didn't exist before. It's all born out of Make, Market, Launch IT," he explains.

Colin's long-term vision involves creating a passive income stream out of the final incarnation of this online business model. He wants to be able to travel with his wife and sustain a lifestyle as a "digital nomad," running his business from a laptop anywhere in the world with working Wi-Fi.

He's excited by the possibilities. "The end result will not be an hour's work for an hour's pay, and that's very compelling. That's what keeps me going."

Make, Market, Launch IT, he believes, is the key to getting there. "If you have an aspiration to earn a passive income and take what you know, to package it so that you can have a passive income, then go for it. This is the opportunity."

Make, Market, Launch IT also gave him a new distinction regarding success in the information product market. "What I've learned is the actual difference isn't in the product. The difference is in the way the product is marketed. You've got to have a good product, but if you have a great product and your marketing isn't any good, you're not going anywhere."

However, after going through the program and building his initial product, he has begun sharing this knowledge with others who have hired him as a consultant. "I've already had a few people approach me to say, 'Can you help me?'" he says. "And I've earned income from that as well."

His parting advice to other creators? "Set a big goal, step up to it. Especially if what you can package is making a difference to other people's lives, I mean, what a great way to go about spending your time."

Colin has now opened up his advanced mind power training suite of tools to a wide audience and continues to develop his suite of training products through AdvancedMindPowerTraining.com

"Somewhere, something incredible is
waiting to be known."

—Carl Sagan

In Closing: One Final Gift
to Change Your Life

"You changed my life."

After our combined 40+ years of creating products in every format you can imagine, those four words are still our greatest reward, bar none. Those words fuel our passion. They drive our creative process. They give us a visceral thrill of excitement—and they leave us in a peak of joy.

We hope this book inspires you to take on a new role, as a teacher, a leader and a visionary—or to raise yourself to a new level of achievement along this path. As you accept this new position, you step into a truly unique and powerful gift: that of transformation. As you pass this gift on to your students, your clients, your friends and your loved ones, we hope you feel the same abundance of joy, passion and excitement that we do.

You've earned it—and you deserve it.

As you're sharing this gift with others, we encourage you to share one more gift with yourself. It's a small gift, but it's a significant one that can create a seismic shift in your entrepreneurial journey.

Give yourself the gift of urgency.

We know that you have a lot of priorities. You may have a partner. You may have a family. You may even be working another job as you get this business off the ground.

However, you've invested enough of your energy to make it this far, which says to us that you're incredibly committed to an entrepreneurial future.

Honor that commitment by making your product—and the business around it—a priority.

You may have only one chance to transform the life of a customer or client. Stay focused on these results. Stay focused on creating a business around it and stay focused on realizing your vision at the highest level— always with a sense of urgency.

We've seen the power that this commitment has had on our customers, some of whom you've met in this book. They were once in your shoes, looking at the same opportunity you're considering today. It's here in front of you now. If you reach out and take it, the possibilities are limitless. Take it from us.

Neither one of us could have predicted where our journeys would lead. We're so grateful for the milestones we've reached, the products we've created, the relationships we've fostered—and the lives we've changed.

In fact, gratitude can't fully express it. That's why we've made it our mission to pass it on, to empower people like you to do what we've done and turn your expertise, experience, perspective and good old-fashioned know-how into a valuable product that changes people's lives.

As we finish this book with you, we hope it marks the start of your journey, from wherever you are now toward the fullest expression of your vision. We're incredibly grateful to you for trusting your time to us. We're also incredibly excited to see what you come up with. In fact, we can't wait.

We also hope this marks the start of *our* journey together. If you'd like to continue your discovery of turning your expertise into a product you can sell—and building a real business around that product—please visit us at our website, **MakeMarketLaunch.com**.

As we've shown you, there's an incredible opportunity in the marketplace right now to significantly improve your value, bring in new revenue streams and create a lasting legacy. Don't wait to take action. The right time is *now*.

Until then, thank you for making us a part of your entrepreneurial journey.

We look forward to working with you again—and we wish you all the joy, delight and excitement of making the impact on the world that's both your gift and your birthright.

Please visit us at MakeMarketLaunch.com for your free video series on how to turn your ideas into income. We'll share our best, cutting-edge strategies for creating a product from scratch, or maximizing a product you already have, but that may not be producing the income or impact you desire.

3830 Valley Centre Drive #705-314
San Diego, CA 92130

866.654.6534
858.720.8720

http://www.MakeMarketLaunch.com

18721348R00089

Made in the USA
Charleston, SC
17 April 2013